THE LION BRIDGE

ALSO BY MICHAEL PALMER

POETRY BOOKS AND CHAPBOOKS

At Passages
An Alphabet Underground
For a Reading
Sun
Songs for Sarah
First Figure
Notes for Echo Lake
Alogon
Transparency of the Mirror
Without Music
The Circular Gates
C's Songs
Blake's Newton
Plan of the City of O

SELECTED TRANSLATIONS

Voyelles by Arthur Rimbaud
Jonah Who Will Be 25 in the Year 2000 (film by Alain Tanner)
The Surrealists Look at Art (with Norma Cole)
Blue Vitriol by Alexei Parshchikov (with John High and Michael Molnar)
Theory of Tables by Emmanuel Hocquard
Three Moral Tales by Emmanuel Hocquard
in *The Selected Poetry of Vicente Huidobro*
in *The Random House Book of Twentieth Century French Poetry*
in *Nothing the Sun Could Explain: 20 Contemporary Brazilian Poets*
in *Twenty-two New French Writers*

MICHAEL PALMER

THE LION BRIDGE

*Selected Poems
1972–1995*

A New Directions Book

Author's Note: I would like particularly to thank Lauri Ramey and Michael Davidson for
their editorial advice while assembling this selection. Errors of omission and, above all,
commission remain my responsibility. And to CS, for putting up with it all.

Publisher's Note: Grateful acknowledgment is made to the editors and publishers of the
books in which the poems of *The Lion Bridge* first appeared: *Blake's Newton* (Black
Sparrow Press, 1972); *The Circular Gates* (Black Sparrow Press, 1974); *Without Music* (Black
Sparrow Press, 1977); *Notes for Echo Lake* (North Point Press, 1981); *First Figure* (North
Point Press, 1984); *Sun* (North Point Press, 1988). In addition, the poems of
the last section were originally published in *At Passages* (New Directons, 1995). New
Directions also owes thanks to Eliot Weinberger for his help with this selection.

Manufactured in the United States of America
New Directions Books are printed on acid-free paper
First published as New Directions Paperbook 855 in 1998
Published simultaneously in Canada by Penguin Books Canada Limited

Library of Congress Cataloging in Publication Data
Palmer, Michael, 1943–
    The Lion bridge : selected poems, 1972–1995 / Michael Palmer.
        p.   cm.
    Includes index.
    ISBN 0-8112-1383-8 (alk. paper)
    I. Title.
PS3566.A54A6   1998
811'.54—dc21   97-47579
                                                                    CIP

New Directions Books are published for James Laughlin
by New Directions Publishing Corporation,
80 Eighth Avenue, New York 10011

for Kit, Jean, Clark and Lyn

for Ilya, Arkadii, Nadezhda, Aleksei and Ivan

"crossing the Lion Bridge"

Contents

WITHOUT MUSIC

NOTES FOR ECHO LAKE

FIRST FIGURE

BLAKE'S NEWTON

Its Form

Its form, at tables by fours
leap . . . relieved of their weight.
She turns green
to begin. The Natural History
peregrine, Peale's hawk
is forgetting to talk
like those coast homes
lost in the deeper part.

But to begin a procession
or a succession of lines
replacing the elms whose warps
and curves are called contradictions.

To begin, 'the stamp'
of autumn . . . these parades
whose curved names
folded in as pilgrims.
You start to swim
through a little darkness
and see some trees.

In the New Spring this
snow is the cold
water running off
what it was. The moth
loves the rose but who
does the rose love. It
goes and
around her
dusting some lady's clothes
from an edge like

trees, turning pages, around or
else about her, the wings marked
by eyes, and seeing twice.

Speech (Across Time)

"If, instead of whispering . . ."

The tract of voice
now in wave form.
Relative energy, decibels
a woman's rising
pitch clearly graphed.
"A stream of sound"
or jags of a large crowd
laughing. Spectrum
of harmonics; sound
pulls on sequent sound
as 'my name.' Sing
'a' [a] as in 'far.'

Holy Tuesday
bright with haze,
the Duke came.
Six oz. of bread.

Saturday:
San Piero.

Tuesday (Kalends):
the dry wind,
dinner with B—.

Thursday:
alone, the snow
not melting.
Twelve oz. at noon.

Friday:
head of the old man,
the raised arm,
dinner alone.

Monday:
legs of the lower figure,
the last of it.

Thursday 13TH
(Corpus Domini):
the blue field,
dinner with B—.

Monday: colder,
the child's torso.
Moon through the first quarter.

A Reasoned Reply to Gilbert Ryle

(After Blake's Newton)

Sound becomes difficult
to dispose of

etc. You go to sit down
and hope for a chair.

One of a pair of
eyes

distends.
Redness begins

on the left side.
The car always starts

in the morning
and it takes me

where someone else
is supposed to be

going
twice each week.

Or else the problem
of light and air.

Upstairs a small leak.
Trouble through the other

eye
which stays open

unless the window itself
is broken.

For L.Z.

A reasonable ear
in music, Bottom,
let's have it
out of tongs
and bones, was it
tongues? "To gather"
or "to ring";
and damp bones
below the stone
arches, a man's jaw
displayed on dark paper
as the bridge came down
following the song.

Figure
the gammadion
formed of four capital
gammas
in a cross
or voided Greek cross
the same gammadion
the gamma she reads
meaning cornerstone.

Once in October
not seeing
the Gegenschein
or counterglow
an elliptical light
opposite the sun
and near the ecliptic
in Sagittarius the centaur
'diurnal archer.'

A Vitruvian Figure by Juan Gris

begins with a line from Donne
or anyone, that drawes Natures workes
from Natures law
moving from the eyes and spare
features this time a woman's figure
defining a circle compressed
where the arms are too weak to extend.

Each day some features change.
The mirror with its own columns
and rosettes at each corner
has a yellow frame
where the Crucian beads are hanging,
but her own body in the diagram
tells two different times

that are constant
like the dots and irregular
curves the oval encloses
the way Gris painted it
at twenty-nine, supposedly
building up forms from
the separate parts, from the eyes
and empty features to the rounded
shoulders, the curve at the saddle
of bony hips, and the legs
spread wide marking
the limits of the ring.

Prose 9

Prose 9 is about the space between the
i and the v in 5. A donut approxi-
mation of the full moon appears be-
hind the central part of The Great Forest.
The entire city of trees lies in ruins
but the bird doesn't know it. It's
green but seems to be a city rather than
trees or else the remains of either one.
The sky is more grey than blue in
1927 and the boardwalk has fallen
leaving a mountain.

THE CIRCULAR GATES

from The Brown Book

But do we interpret the words
before obeying the order
—The Brown Book

for . . .

This is difficult but not impossible: coffee
childhood; in the woods there's a bird;
its song stops you and makes you blush
and so on; it's her
small and dead behind the roses
better left alone; we wander around the park
and out of our mouths come blood and smoke
and sounds; small children and giants
young mothers and big sisters
will be walking in circles next to the water

Men without arms their heads in a box
I'm sailing the black boat and want you to watch
it cross. The imaginary animals
circle the water. Four legs dance
in a clam. I love the blueness of the water
and how the figures ("the pale bodies") bend
toward transparency, so that it becomes harder
from here to see them clearly
and to distinguish what seems to be
the beginning of the story from the end

The heron is riding
on a porcupine's back
and two apples hang

from the unicorn's horn
What is the name of
the Peregrine Falcon

What is the name
of the Ring-necked Duck
or the green-winged bird

perched upside down
in the hollow of a tree
or the bird with a human body

and a naked man in its beak
And why did he build a machine
allowing him to breathe

all night but never to speak
Copper then red then brown
The owl's eye gathers in light

at the center of the fountain
The first and last of
the animals surround him

from The Book Against Understanding

To learn what to say to unlearn
The order of islands here

The number of fingers
made from ideas

certain   Bulgaria   anywhere
grounds   stairway   statement

normal   nature   cases
Visitors from the Dog Star

filling up the house
Words for *are* and *were not*

If I knew it it's what I thought
If I knew it it's what I thought

If I knew it it's what I thought
it was

The order of islands here
If you take it

will I give it back
at two o'clock

Will you hold it
in my hand

And the relation to an eyelid
by the quantity of light

As in
His story's impossible to read

As in
We'll see it just in time

whenever we find it
missing

As if by saying "morning" on January 8th
the light would be set forward
along the megalophonous shore

Was there anything else you wanted to know
about the body where I belong
how the torso is cut off from a waving arm

by the yellow space in the background
and how the head has been put on wrong
or not wrong. Each looked into the water

and was frightened by a different thing
of his or her own making
One was frightened by stripes

and the other by a turtle
even though I knew it wouldn't bite
but would take me for a ride

It was the time when the phone always rings
to dissolve the mediating scene
in which a phone always rings

to help us with our counting
I say hello to the lateral darkness
who answers guardedly

in painted fragments. The drop of a hat
If the shoe fits. A thin bird flaps
before it sits. Who answers noiselessly

Hans Memling is watching from my matchbox
where the serpent lives
This is his nest

In the Empire of Light
the water's completely dry

floating on a surface of itself
around islands pointed south-southwest

The wind fills it then
with more of itself

according to the rules
which cause parallel lines

to vibrate and cross
less and less

among the hanging baskets from a rain forest
among the visiting statesmen

from a rain forest
Here the dancer stops

to regain her balance
and reelaborate the distance

from the feet to the head
The risk is a part of the rhythm

She steps out of
and into balance

with those who are left
Chalk-marks show them where to stand

He stopped part way across the field to
sit down and rest. An eagle
descended from the sky and an angel with the face of death

Before I had a name
I came out of a place where there wasn't a door
holding my breath

in slippery hands. Door to wall
and back again. The things these were
The modified currents of air

at which the dancers are taught to stare
whenever they turn
to go but instead fall over

at the idea of taking an ordinary walk
for example to the Post Office
or a restaurant. And all the original atoms

of water and skin
we think we can find there
if we try. This is not Alaska

and the sun-dial
is not the sun secretly dying
during the night

from Series

Prose 22

Plan of the City of O. The great square
curves down toward the cathedral. The
water runs out into night where the patron
saint still maintains his loft. He enters
from the lower level and pulls up the ladder
after him. The women and children and
most of the old men spend their time painting
pictures of the ladder. The rest lay the
three kinds of stone or type the performance
for the eastern quarter. There the first
colony left its box-shaped mark. But
the sun always goes down in several places,
so the clocks serve as maps. And at the
end of the nearest mountain stands the
larger and less perfect box.

Prose 31

The Logic of Contradictions

A logical principle is said to be an empty
or formal proposition because it can add
nothing to the premises of the argument it
governs. This leads to the logic of contra-
dictions. It is an anacoluthon to say that
a proposition is impossible because it is
self-contradictory. (It is also ambiguous.)
The definition of the possible as that which
in a given state of information (real or
pretended) we do not know not to be true
conceals another anacoluthon.

Sonnet:

Now I see them

Now I see them sitting me before a mirror.
There's noise and laughter. Somebody
mentions that hearing is silver
before we move on to Table One
with the random numbers. I look down
a long street containing numbers.
A white four leans against the fence
and disappears. In the doorway
is the seven, then the x
painted red so you can find it
more easily. Five goes by
without its cap. My father wears
the second x. He has a grey cloud
for a face, and dark lines for arms.

from Chinese Hours

The End of the Ice Age and Its Witnesses

Yesterday your fever returned
It was near the middle of July

and we went to see the Red king
Then I took out the net

together with the red bird
and put it down

on the bank of the river. Could the
flat milling stone and a

subsistence on seeds be originally
an American invention? We

cuddled on the seat of the car
until she said desperately

I was never unhappier;
then I told them that we wished to

continue our journey
because we were not reaching our destination

at all. But the creatures of this island
were very kind. The sky

was a deep green, without clouds
since the rain had been falling regularly

onto the lowest branch of a tamarack
where we hung by our knees. Considering

the look of the trees
we were somewhere in Canada

or the Northeast: flat, blue-green needles
0.8 to 1.3 inches long

that yellow in the fall; ovoid cones,
bark thin, scaly and

gray to reddish brown. The soil
is moist and spongy

under the car. E
is white like fog, and A dark,

cycles at some future time
to tell about—

the white tents in the primer
and the kind of flower that trembles easily—

Nothing of the sort is known
or probable on this side of the ocean

nor is there any early record of tents
On a given evening for example

they're playing cards
at the bottom of a swamp or pond; the Tartar

deserts light up; by the stairways
and armchairs of the rocks a

small world, pale and flat
"is coming to understand itself"

Third Symmetrical Poem

Were you listening and
did you hear them
In the question
some of the trees bend
The circle and the light

resembled an entire body
taken from the light
a body of wires and
a body with no inside
It was her voice that made

the sky acutest at its vanishing
the same as it would be
the weight of air
that turned the apparent form
into an empty bowl

that before had held water
The bowl imitates motion
by moving around
I don't know at all
how you get from two to one

except by walking upside down
with your head partly underground
If you start from the beginning
of the evening
you can see the leaves

on the ground
If you start from the opening
of the letter
you can watch the letters following each other
If you start with the picture

you get a prohibition
If you start with the face
you get a complex modulation
of the eyes and teeth
If you start with the darkness

you get the forest
which is dark
the wires which are sometimes not
then the window and the photograph
of the painting of the face

Fourth Symmetrical Poem

A book with lines through the words cannot be read
but if you take one out then two are left
the prévoyant said, and did
in regard to the hole in his neck
that had not been cut there without ill effect
It rained again that night deep inside
where only recently had occurred the abandonment of signs

Dream-hours though take less time
in whose use the impression made on us
by the signs played no part, in which
there was no such thing as understanding
in the sense of such an impression
In this case one might say "Only
in the system has the sign any life"

and still be mistaken
sometime during the night
It continued to rain. Still
if the train does not arrive
punctually at five o'clock
was it also the impression
that he might miss some connexion

Things continue to drain, a mixture
of red and white
from the partly improvised pipe
But those which seemed to propose a certain meaning
would almost always be completely changed by evening
of the same day, even when carefully composed
in the standard procedural way

so that there at least appeared to be some kind of flow
Just this gesture has been made accessible
as an accompaniment to hearing
First it rains and then the vast
armies of the plain begin to sing
a strange song with
some help from the telephone

It's easy to say that the future was already gone
by then because of the flames
and this may or may not be wrong
Certainly no one wanted to name names
in case they included their own
Certainly there was nothing
in one sense to be done

for Michael Davidson

Fifth Symmetrical Poem

The way the future uses up blood and light
and the individual marks are altered every day

until you reach the end of the row of trees
It has to be possible to imagine these

infinitely extended
and to walk by in a curved line

remembering the pencil that draws the line
putting the water on one side

and agreeing that the chair will be white
Each day each letter of the previous day

would be replaced by the next one in line
and the Z by an A

of the same size and shape. I dream that I say
It's raining

and it has no meaning
I dream that she's waking

in the white chair
Everyone we know is here

Or when you covered the numbers
no sounds seemed clear

We would come and go
on hands and feet

We would move them
to get somewhere

WITHOUT MUSIC

For Voice

A little faithful to the dream mirror
A little faceless in the dream mirror
and followed by zeroes
how many to the head of each pin

how many to the hexagon
starry night of balancing
but of careless balancing
between identical windows

one to open one to stay closed
The figure unconscious in the leather chair
will wake up and leave
eventually, will wake up and stare

in amazement
never before having slept
Here white ones and white
ones are dancing

in particulate ones
always five to the hexagon
plus a minus equal to one
a small river lost

in thought, perfect late
nineteenth-century voyage
to the bookstore and back
curved line a finger

would describe in air
Here the Pacific
meets the Sea of Cortez
to form a desert. This is the corner

and this is the order in which we wept
six-sided tears
lovely the ironwork overhead
lovely the dome

of Montaner you showed us
in a book. Now letter and word
have begun to disappear
the *A* no longer drawn

with three remembered strokes
but shaping itself
a little confused in the way
people conceive the possibility

as theoretical, so many feathers
to so many pounds
so many objects unidentified
will force so many witnesses

to stop their cars and watch
will cause so many dogs to bark
from the endlessly burning house
These are the toys of Dionysus

top, rattle, bone-dice and mirror
Thus farmers have nothing to eat
Thus Ocean began marriage
by wedding his sister

and Sun will never transgress his measures
lest he be found out
It's better it says to hide ignorance
We must not act and speak

as if asleep
Eye precedes ear

Tomb of Baudelaire

At the end of the bridge is a state of prison. Then
it goes back into my throat drying my throat.

Miracle of Sicilian weeping. Bleeds in one of his many
dreams.

He announced that he was about to give a free 'poetry
suicide'—a free 'poultry recital.' Everyone be-
lieved him.

———————

At the end of the bridge is a state of prison. A
voyage will hide itself in your heart, bleeding from the
left eye, the organ of sight. A voyage will hide
itself in someone unfamiliar like a heap of salt.
Mingled with the ordinary blueness would be waves of
foreheads shaped like cups.

She thought he could hear her.

To dance is to live.

———————

Calm and order of an autumn sky. At the end of a
bridge is the state of prison, voyage of eye and
throat full of the fear of night. Then all of winter
will enter like a red block, or like the calm and
order of an autumn sky.

139. Change of form. 139a. Change of colour.

122. Pitfalls. 136. Covers with a lid.

———————

It doesn't matter what you say but how you say it. By
pronouncing the words they become different. It comes
from above (pointing to his head). Then it goes all
sorts of ways down. Then it goes back into my throat
drying my throat.

Tonight it's a certainty that the President will resign
('a virtual certainty').

After the party they drove back to her house where she
sucked him off while he spoke to someone on the tele-
phone about the possibility of a job.

————

Plato's warning against telling stories, *mython
tina diēgeisthai.*

Or the certainty of the ten fingers and ten feet. You
laugh a lot because during the first phase someone
who has taken hasheesh is 'gifted with a marvelous
comic sense' which contains its own opposite like the
end of a bridge.

The verb divides us evenly into two objects.

————

A pretty girl is like a melody.

You must be more confident now that you've won the
prize.

And if you listen. And if you listen hearing, if you
listen thought. I've been thinking about the whole
trouble about how I got lost in the woods. A man my-
self is lying in a house. Or alone among myself answering
a house. To be calm and voluptuous conjuring a house.
To be eligible for the house. If you listen image, if you

listen house. Ordinary calm and order of the house. Coffee comma parentheses. Coffee parentheses order. Coffee parentheses coffee. 131. Untrodden. 136. Covers with a lid.

––––––––––

137. Combination. 138. Arrangement.

Plato's admonition against telling stories about being, *mython tina diēgeisthai.*

Dear Apollinaire: We drove 500 miles to attend the wedding of a relative. Our son was to be in the bridal party. The wedding was to take place at 4 p.m. on Saturday. On the Friday night before the wedding, the bride and groom got into a fight and the groom broke the bride's nose so the wedding was canceled.

What do we do with the wedding gift we were going to take to the church? Who pays for the tuxedo our son rented for the occasion and never got to wear? And how about the motel bill?

The Library is Burning

(Eighth Symmetrical Poem)

The library is burning floor by floor
delivering pictures from liquid to sleep

as we roll over thinking to run
A mistaken anticipation has led us here

to calculate the duration of a year
in units of aloe and wood

But there will be no more dust in corners
and no more dogs appearing through dust

to question themselves uncertainly
Should it finally be made clear

that there's no cloud inside no body
no streetlamps, no unfoldings at five o'clock

along the edge of a curved path
Masters of the present tense

greet morning from their cautious beds
while the greater masters of regret

change water into colored glass
The stirrings are the same and different

The stirrings are the same and different
and secretly the same

The fear of winter is the fear of fire
disassembling winter

and that time the message was confused
it felt the most precise

Ninth Symmetrical Poem

(after Southwell)

It's November the thirty-third
of an actual November
and the children sleep in the crystal world
turning their heads from the fire that burns them

The burning children are invisible
but the carriers of wounded thought
are everywhere visible
as letters strung along a word

whose economies
work backward from speech
Mirrored we reflect such things
as they've seen

Dance of the Bees (September)

As the sun's
       light caught in a mirror
       or held by water . . .

To walk with bees under the earth's heel

shadowed by light
and corrected by light. The hard sweetness sticks

to your throat
a little more each day

meaning somewhat less. In love's presence
it's advised to go to the track

wearing love's best flowering hat
Greet royalty with a vacant smile

Greet the revolution with obvious respect
Keep your fingers to yourself

but display the revolution's naked wrists
Distill memory between linen sheets

Avoid all suicide pacts

On the Way to Language

The answer was
the sun, the question

of all the fragrances undressed
by the rats in the Pentagon

is Claude's, little
memory jars

empty of their pickled plums
and the tiny

pile of dried bodies under the floorboard
(we had to sell that car)

Summers are always difficult
arriving too soon, too

much wind and the absolute
darkness when it finally descends

over the plantation. We're not ashamed
of our immense wealth

even somewhat proud
of the cleanliness of the servants' quarters

From the sound of their weeping
they seem happy enough

in their work, childlike
and contrite. The answer was

memory, an efficient
engine driven by earthly

remains and the question
of the valley of desire

crossed by the bridge
of frequent sighs

Tenth Symmetrical Poem

A dream in imperfect alexandrines
Through night's eye those tending the book move
as surds or signs, the cooks with their guns
and soldiers with their aprons and copper pots
define archē and telos, passages

translucent as
the old Stalinist says
dolphins in their course, the forest is
hazardous, 'familiar,' its hidden
events. Through night's eye those tending the

book peer out
on a scene from a book
while we who have been translated
(who are waiting to be translated)
do not

Without Music

Les lettres qui formaient des mots artificiels
Reverdy

Small sun against the lower edge licking us
She showed me her tongue coated with thorns

A careful life of stars in a redwood box

times labor's loss not mine
based upon the loss itself, 'not mine'

. . . formed such words imperfectly bodied

as empty sleep weighed against dream
bodies and parts of bodies distributed

according to given laws
                         across a field
Who could help but love the equations

night's music hung from each line
the headless man looks at the quarter moon

and the moon watches the man
resting invisible beneath a tree

luminous city   sounds that pour
from the center of a courtyard

where we watch ourselves talk
This poem is called Rebuilding the House

Crossing the Hill

Queens and kings of the perilous edge
of an alphabet we
are are we this
faithful cat crossing the hill

to where time sits
in its midday likeness
or ordinary dark time
like an alphabet

dancing the straight-forward dance
Egypt lives in certain cats
who refuse to scratch
and refuse to sit

here where Egypt lives
as an alphabet
of visible undertakings
mistaken for an actual cat

who is the opposite of an alphabet
geometrical and abstract
and alive because of that
How long will the dry time last

beneath the hill
the serious speakers ask
have the makers unbuilt all this
to decorate a hill

for A.M.

The Meadow

Resembling a meadow
'folded in all thought'
a lamp is lit only vaguely remembered
for its form, an elephant
of pale blue porcelain
with trunk curved upward
lighting a room   a gift
toward a featureless room
whose walls are lined with children's books
whose readers are unable to read

for Robert Duncan

NOTES FOR ECHO LAKE

The Comet

"An outlook based upon philosophy became obligatory."
Bruno Schulz

That year the end of winter stood under a sign
All days were red in the margin
writ large against the ochre rooftops
                              and yes that was your father's

face, a murder best forgotten
by passersby inured to the dust
though blinded a bit by the redness
                              Invisible charges rose

in the poles, only
to enclose them, a parody of juggling
within the lap of eternal matter
                              like love c. mid-afternoon

eyes half-open, adjustments
at an unexpected point of the experiment
occurred toward the backstage of things
                                        warm

currents of air and some really
depressing tricks that filled one
with true melancholy
                    regarding *principium individuationis*

suitable more to the success of an idea
in an illustrated journal
of modern physics
                    splendidly bogus

and immediately satisfying
as forecast long ago by the prophets
in a circus farce

Notes for Echo Lake   1

"I am glad to see you Ion."

He says this red as dust, eyes a literal self among selves and picks the coffee up.

Memory is kind, a kindness, a kind of unlistening, a grey wall even toward which you move.

It was the woman beside him who remarked that he never looked anyone in the eye. (This by water's edge.)

This by water's edge.

And all of the song 'divided into silences', or 'quartered in three silences'.

Dear Charles, I began again and again to work, always with no confidence as Melville might explain. Might complain.

A message possibly intercepted, possibly never written. A letter she had sent him.

But what had his phrase been exactly, "Welcome to the Valley of Tears," or maybe "Valley of Sorrows." At least one did feel welcome, wherever it was.

A kind of straight grey wall beside which they walk, she the older by a dozen years, he carefully unlistening.

Such as words are. A tape for example a friend had assembled containing readings by H.D., Stein, Williams, others. Then crossing the bridge to visit Zukofsky, snow lightly falling.

Breaking like glass Tom had said and the woman from the island. Regaining consciousness he saw first stars then a face leaning over him and heard the concerned voice, "Hey baby you almost got *too* high."

Was was and is. In the story the subject disappears.

They had agreed that the sign was particular precisely because arbitrary and that it included the potential for (carried the sign of) its own dissolution, and that there was a micro-syntax below the order of the sentence and even of the word, and that in the story the subject disappears it never disappears. 1963: only one of the two had the gift of memory.

Equally one could think of a larger syntax, e.g. the word-as-book proposing always the book-as-word. And of course still larger.

Beginning and ending. As a work begins and ends itself or begins and rebegins or starts and stops. Ideas as elements of the working not as propositions of a work, even in a propositional art. (Someone said someone thought.)

That is, snow
    a) is
    b) is not
      falling—check neither or both.

If one lives in it. 'Local' and 'specific' and so on finally seeming less interesting than the 'particular' wherever that may locate.

"What I really want to show here is that it is not at all clear *a priori* which are the simple colour concepts."

Sign that empties itself at each instance of meaning, and how else to reinvent attention.

Sign that empties . . . That is *he* would ask *her.* He would be the asker and she unlistening, nameless mountains in the background partly hidden by cloud.

The dust of course might equally be grey, the wall red, our memories perfectly accurate. A forest empty of trees, city with no streets, a man having swallowed his tongue. As there is no 'structure' to the sentence and no boundary or edge to the field in question. As there is everywhere no language.

As I began again and again, and each beginning identical with the next, meaning each one accurate, each a projection, each a head bending over the motionless form.

And he sees himself now as the one motionless on the ground, now as the one bending over. Lying in an alley between a house and a fence (space barely wide enough for a body), opening his eyes he saw stars and heard white noise followed in time by a face and a single voice.

Now rain is falling against the south side of the house but not the north where she stands before a mirror.

"Don't worry about it, he's already dead."

"Te dérange pas, il est déjà mort."

"È morto lei, non ti disturba."

She stands before the mirror touches the floor. Language reaches for the talk as someone falls. A dead language opens and opens one door.

So here is color. Here is a color darkening or color here is a darkening. Here white remains . . .

And you indicate the iris of the portrait's eye, a specific point on the iris, wanting that color as your own. There is a grey wall past which we walk arm in arm, fools if we do greater fools if we don't.

And I paint the view from my left eye, from the balcony of the eye overlooking a body of water, an inland sea possibly, possibly a man-made lake.

And do I continue as the light changes and fades, eventually painting in pitch dark. That is, if you write it has it happened twice:

It rained again that night deep inside
where only recently had occurred the abandonment of signs

Portrait Now Before Then

That is A, that is Anna speaking. That is A, that is no one speaking and it's winter. That is a bridge and a bridge of winter pure as talk.

The river is red.

I'm offering a name.

The river begins between sheer cliffs. There are parts of words in it.

What he heard was winter talking.

I'm erasing one name.

Here is A in a story of first things, things first seen as they were speaking, fire before water and a sun that's one foot wide.

That is A crossing a bridge and a letter is that which it says it is. One A means winter. Casey Daedalus survived the war.

———————

In his dream the bell rings and rings until she wakes to a perfect copy of herself as a polished stone falling from a lighted window toward the welcoming arms of the crowd below.

In his dream the robed and bearded men stand beneath the letter-tree. I hold out my left arm and read the word 'cloud' as it appears there. She shows me the tiny butterfly painted on the back of her hand. By then we have become the four weeping men.

———————

In the *Comprehensive Treatise on Naked Skin* he reads that the occasional dark spots are not blemishes but characteristic features of the Victorian glaze.

The light narrows to a light above a door and the world grows, briefly, cold. Reading the eyes glaze, a bell summons winter from our sleep.

We stumbled over shards of rose-quartz across hills where nothing remained, hills where nothing had been left. We visit those hills from which.

In his dream he sees himself as a name, hears an identical name and recalls four words each day. In A's dream a crowd is whispering.

––––––––

What do the letters spell.

Once he walked on the frozen common and once a dog found him.

Probing the heart for ways of grace, yellow, purple and white flowering on the same stalk.

And once he lay face down in snow and that became the dream.

What do the letters mean.

An A is an ending in full sun, another resembles its shadow, and the third is that which it says it is. They entered tired and wet.

As each wheel of meeting turns in a wheel, each letter is spoken to begin. For an entire year the river was dry, but the following spring it poured through the streets.

He wondered about the terms, what they called 'parts of speech', and the words one couldn't say. Everything had what was known as 'its place'.

House of mud or house of stone and the crowd with outstretched arms. At dawn gulls gather on rooftops. Things try to stand for other things. I'm coming to the age I am.

Notes for Echo Lake   2

He would assume a seeing into the word, whoever was there to look. Would care to look. A coming and going in smoke.

A part and apart.

Voices through a wall. They are there because we hear them what do we hear. The pitch rises toward the end to indicate a question.

What's growing in the garden.

To be at a loss for words. How does the mind move there, walking beside the bank of what had been a river. How does the light.

And rhythm as an arm, rhythm as the arm extended, he turns and turns remembering the song. What did she recall.

It was of course the present the sibyl most clearly saw, reading the literal signs, the words around her, until a further set of signs appeared. And to divine the fullness of the message she uttered would demand of her listener an equivalent attention. The message was the world translated, and speaker and listener became one. Her message was the sign itself.

Hermes alike as the bearer and concealer. Hermes as the sign.

Who lives in the speaking and unlistening, wild onions by the river, roses in the garden a hundred years old, lilac, iris, poppy, jasmine trellised above the kitchen window.

They walk beside departure and images of a dry riverbed unfold, voices through a wall arm in arm. They walk beside an answer typing each letter as it appears. A large white room has a beamed ceiling. The poor live in long rows.

While staring at the sea he paints a woman's face, requests more light and time. Is there ever an image that appears, word inside word, skin blue as dust, nameless hills beyond. Is there an image if there is.

To be at a loss and to return there, saying things and speaking, it's started to rain. He paints a woman's face the color of the sea but portrays someone else as an empty chair. Then he learns to erase four words each day.

As an arm folded might mean 'to flow.'

They collide near the cafe door, smile politely and pass. He watches the philosopher turn the corner and disappear.

There is agreeable poetry.

There is poetry like a white cloth.

There's a poetry licking its tongue.

Let me lend you my fork.

Voice occurs through a wall.

As song divides itself, she explains with a wave.

We have never been happy here have never been happier.

Notes for Echo Lake   3

Words that come in smoke and go.

Some things he kept, some he kept and lost. He loved the French poets
fell through the partly open door.

And I as it is, I as the one but less than one in it. I was the blue against
red and a voice that emptied, and I is that one with broken back.

While April is ours and dark, as something always stands for
what is: dying elm, headless man, winter—
$\qquad\qquad\qquad\qquad\qquad$ salamander, chrysalis,

fire—
$\qquad$ grammar and silence.

Or grammar against silence. Years later they found themselves talking
in a crowd. Her white cat had been killed in the woods behind her
house. It had been a good possibly even a terrible winter. Ice had
coated the limbs of the hawthorn and lilac, lovely but dangerous. Travel
plans had been made then of necessity abandoned. At different times
entire weeks had seemed to disappear. She wondered what initially
they had agreed not to discuss.

Some things he kept while some he kept apart.

As Robert's call on Tuesday asking whether I knew that Zukofsky had
died a couple of days before. The call came as I was reading a copy of
Larry Rivers' talk at Frank O'Hara's funeral (July, 1966), "He was a
quarter larger than usual. Every few inches there was some sewing
composed of dark blue thread. Some stitching was straight and three
or four inches long, others were longer and semi-circular . . ."

As Robert's call on Tuesday a quarter larger than usual asking whether I
knew whether I knew. Blue thread every few inches, straight and semi-
circular, and sand and wet snow. Blue snow a couple of days before.
Whether I know whatever I know.

The letters of the words of our legs and arms. What he had seen or thought he'd seen within the eye, voices overheard rising and falling. And if each conversation has no end, then composition is a placing beside or with and is endless, broken threads of cloud driven from the west by afternoon wind.

The letters of the words of our legs and arms. In the garden he dreamt he saw four bearded men and listened to them discussing metaphor. They are standing at the points of the compass. They are standing at the points of the compass and saying nothing. They are sitting in the shade of a flowering tree. She is holding the child's body out toward the camera. She is standing before the mirror and asking. She is offering and asking. He-she is asking me a question I can't quite hear. Evenings they would walk along the shore of the lake.

Letters of the world. Bright orange poppy next to white rose next to blue spike of larkspur and so on. Artichoke crowding garlic and sage. Hyssop, marjoram, orange mint, winter and summer savory, oregano, trailing rosemary, fuchsia, Dutch iris, day lily, lamb's tongue, lamb's ears, blackberry, feverfew, lemon verbena, sorrel, costmary, never reads it as it is, "poet living tomb of his/games."

Eyes eyeing what self never there, as things in metaphor cross, are thrown across, a path he calls the path of names. In the film *La Jetée* she is thrown against time and is marking time:

> sun burns thru the roars
> dear eyes, *all eyes,* pageant
> bay inlet, garden casuarina, spittle-spawn
> (not laurel) nameless we name
> it, and sorrows dissolve—human

In silence he would mark time listening for whispered words. I began this in spring, head ready to burst, flowers, reddening sky, moon with a lobster, New York, Boston, return, thin coating of ice, moon while dogs bark, moon dogs bark at, now it's late fall.

And now he told me it's time to talk.

Words would come in smoke and go, inventing the letters of the voyage, would walk through melting snow to the corner store for cigarettes, oranges and a newspaper, returning by a different route past red brick townhouses built at the end of the Civil War. Or was the question in the letters themselves, in how by chance the words were spelled.

In the poem he learns to turn and turn, and prose seems always a sentence long.

Fals

efore
must
re

The   cent
rain y   o count
first mi.   hours then trees

rocks, windows, mailboxes, streetlights
and pictographs refusing to
rest even for the brief span it

would take to dry off, change clothes and
reemerge grotesque yet oddly
attractive like Paganini

whose mother was visited by
a seraph in Genoa not
long before his birth and who is

thought now to have acquired much of
his technical wizardry as
a result of Marfan's syndrome

a quite common anomaly
of the connective tissues which
may well account for the tall and

angular body, muscular
underdevelopment as well
as the hypermobile joints that

eventuated on the stage
in a peculiar stance, a
spectacular bowing technique

and an awesome mastery of
the fingerboard. He would bring his
left hip forward to support his

body's weight. His left shoulder, thrust
forward also, would enable
him to rest his left elbow on

his chest, a buttress against the
stress of forceful bowing along
with debilitating muscle

fatigue. The looseness of the right
wrist and shoulder gave pliancy
leading to broad acrobatic

bowing. The 'spider' fingers of
his left hand permitted a range
on the fingerboard which many

attributed to black magic
for Paganini was said to
have signed a pact with Lucifer

to acquire virtuosity
as a small child. After his death
perhaps due in part to this tale

in part also to rumours of
gambling and wild debauchery
the Church refused to allow him

burial on hallowed ground. In
consequence his body was moved
furtively from place to place

until after many years and
for reasons still mysterious
the Church finally relented.

A few paradoxes should be
noted as an afterword. Though
accused of charlatanism he

was rewarded for his skill like
no one before him. He loved his
violin above all yet once

he gambled it away at cards.
He accepted wealth and renown
from his worshipping admirers

but tripled the admission price
to his concerts in the face of
adverse reviews. While openly

irreverent of tradition
he still took a princess as his lover
and let nations strike medals in his name.

To Robert E. Symmes 1933
for a gift of resemblances

His arm slept. Dream-wounded and a former
figure he wept beside the stream
to see himself becoming it.
Who would write him in as a target
burned by the sun
who heard a name he would become
or once was, red
as a second following dawn? The city
is full of ones called us
who endlessly greet each other by a name
that changes each time.
It's a wonder to return, head aching,
to witness the bear to its rest
and it's odd to wake and rewrite it
as a kind of resemblance.
I am tired and would like to leave.
I have never been here. The book
wears a lion's mane. For a moment
they were visitors resembling themselves.
Laughing he had said, I am tired of this waiting to be born.
The ones called figures crowd the street.
Each is missing part of his name
and each longs to be drawn a face.

11 v 79

Notes for Echo Lake   4

Who did he talk to

Did she trust what she saw

Who does the talking

Whose words formed awkward curves

Did the lion finally talk

Did the sleeping lion talk

Did you trust a north window

What made the dog bark

What causes a grey dog to bark

What does the juggler tell us

What does the juggler's redness tell us

Is she standing in an image

Were they lost in the forest

Were they walking through a forest

Has anything been forgotten

Did you find it in the dark

Is that one of them new atomic-powered wristwatches

Was it called a talking song

Is that an oblong poem

Was poetry the object

Was there once a road here ending at a door

Thus from bridge to bridge we came along

Did the machine seem to talk

Did he read from an empty book

Did the book grow empty in the dark, grey felt hat blowing down the
street, arms pumping back and forth, legs slightly bowed

Are there fewer ears than songs

Did he trust a broken window

Did he wake beneath a tree in the recent snow

Whose words formed difficult curves

Have the exaggerations quieted down

The light is lovely on trees which are not large

My logic is all in the melting-pot

My life now is very economical

I can say nothing of my feeling about space

Nothing could be clearer than what you see on this wall

Must we give each one a name

Is it true they all have names

Would it not have been simpler

Would it not have been simpler to begin

Were there ever such buildings

I must remember to mention the trees

I must remember to invent some trees

Who told you these things

Who taught you how to speak

Who taught you not to speak

Whose is the voice that empties

Notes for Echo Lake   5

"a blue under people"
Bernadette Mayer, *Memory*

The tree's green explains what a light means, an idea, the bomb or
Donald Duck, a box of marbles in a marble box, the amber jewel
behind the toad's eyes reminds us that it's night. The interpreter of the
text examines the traffic light, coughs and lays the book aside. The dead
mayor sits behind his desk, overcome with wonderment.

The interpreter of a cough examines the light and lays the text aside.
Here and there leaves, clouds, rivers of tears in the streets meant a
sonata for tongues.

Truth to tell the inventor of the code weeps and lays the text aside.
Here and there calendars and walls remind him that it's night, a
sleeping lion is curled up in one corner, a voice can be heard behind a
door, and Plato told us of the law, Plato warned us about the poem. The
dead mayor wonders if the King of France is bald.

Today is an apparent day of empty sleeves and parallelograms, and red
meaning red, and the flag as an object, and red instead of red, the flag
as an object with undulating sides, the spider who taught me to walk,
the emptiness of the code, the spider who forgot how to walk, the
delicate curves within the code, three barking dogs, the mystery of
intervals, the absence of a code, the lion asleep at her feet, the empty
sleeve waving, the bottle now broken, the voices she told him to listen
for, the stolen book, the measurement of intervals.

Does physics know Caesar by name?

Plato warned us of the shadows of the poem, of the words cast against
the wall, and Plato warns against the song.

The tree's green explains what a name means apart from memory, flickers of light in the darkened room, our eyes fixed on the screen on the figures of nothing.

The inventor of the code hears each note and swallows his tongue, frightened by shadows. The lion red as a lobster is green sleeps in one corner dreaming of the hours' numbers and names, a river flowing at his feet. "Shuffle Montgomery" was the song.

And here and there they speak in tongues, correcting the right notes in order to get them wrong. And how many days did you spend underground?

The interpreter of leaves examines each tear as pages turn. In the field at dawn they cross swords and a head rolls while the audience laughs. The dead city listens to the code as it reads, and a poem moves back and forth.

At our feet like a sky the graceful curve. Rumours that they are lovers or were in a previous lifetime made of salt. Hills beyond tipped with snow or salt, a curve broken off, searching for her tongue. A deep blue tasting of salt. The awkward curve and talking cloud, steps toward a forest for want of stairs. Are in a lifetime or were. Rumours that the sender had forgotten the code and swallowed his tongue. A mirror in one corner was about to fall, apparently his memory of Siena and the dome.

And Brother Mouse with parachute in mid-air, forever descending.

That they are figures or were, a pictograph with thumb extended. He drank from an actual glass of beer. An outstretched arm offers me its hand.

Song of the Round Man

(for Sarah when she's older)

The round and sad-eyed man puffed cigars as if
he were alive. Gillyflowers
to the left of the apple, purple bells to the right

and a grass-covered hill behind.
I am sad today said the sad-eyed man
for I have locked my head in a Japanese box

and lost the key.
I am sad today he told me
for there are gillyflowers by the apple

and purple bells I cannot see.
Will you look at them for me
he asked, and tell me what you find?

I cannot I replied
for my eyes have grown sugary and dim
from reading too long by candlelight.

Tell me what you've read then
said the round and sad-eyed man.
I cannot I replied

for my memory has grown tired and dim
from looking at things that can't be seen
by any kind of light

and I've locked my head in a Japanese box
and thrown away the key.
Then I am you and you are me

said the sad-eyed man as if alive.
I'll write you in where I should be
between the gillyflowers and the purple bells

and the apple and the hill
and we'll puff cigars from noon till night
as if we were alive.

Seven Forbidden Words

"Mon chat sur le carreau cherchant une litière"
Baudelaire, 'Spleen'

Who peered from the invisible world
toward a perfectly level field. Terms
will be broken here (have been broken here).
Should a city of blue tile appear
no one will be listening there.
He stood up, walked across the room
and broke his nose against the door.
A was the face of a letter
reflected in the water below.
He watched cross-eyed
learning a few words at a time.
The sun rose behind your shoulder
and told me to act casual
while striking an attitude of studied repose.
You grew these flowers yourself
so how could you forget their names.
The yellow one is said to be uncommon
and the heart tastes as expected, tender
and bitter like an olive
but less violent. It has been summer for a day
or part of a day
with shades drawn. The fires were deliberately set
and the inhabitants welcomed them.

Pre-Petrarchan Sonnet

(after Peter Altenberg)

Someone identical with Dante
sits beside a stone. Enough
is enough is enough of.
It's odd that your hand feels warm
(snow carefully falling).
It's odd that the page was torn
just where the snow had begun.
There was never very much.
There is more (less) than there was.
Today it is 84, 74 and 12
and light and dark.
We are nowhere else.
His smile fell to one side.
Here and there it was very light and dark.

Dear M

Look this figure half-hidden is not a book
This mirror-house is not the book
This photograph conceals a book
I tripped over the flower in the porcelain cup

This shoulder-talk was never a book
She offered a single syllable
This slowness is the book
This spiral is a mark

This mark is no part of it
She rolled over and spoke
I can see from here through something broken
This turning is not a book

This turning from is nothing
The owl is lost within the tree
I tripped over the voice in the porcelain cup
These moths are visitors or were

They are so tired of the book
The pages tell us so
We walked from bridge to bridge
This liquid is clear

and holds no light
A lower voice can be heard
In winter there are eyes
The second thread represents the ear

not listening, the third
the curve of the throat
the fourth the lips and tongue
the fringes of the hair grown long

I remember the name of one color
and I remember the name of the color one
Yes means yet, airs
age and turned telling

The coral benches and tables are empty
The rooftops were painted a useless red
We collected the letters in perfect error
and hurried to unlearn them

The Project of Linear Inquiry

[Let *a* be taken as . . .]
a liquid line beneath the skin
and *b* where the blue tiles meet
body and the body's bridge
a seeming road here, endless

rain pearling light
chamber after chamber
of dust-weighted air
the project of seeing things
so to speak, or things seen

namely a hand, namely
the logic of the hand
holding a bell or clouded lens
the vase perched impossibly near the edge
obscuring the metal tines.

She said "perhaps" then it echoed.
I stood there torn
felt hat in hand
wondering what I had done
to cause this dizziness

"you must learn to live with."
It reveals no identifiable source
(not anyway the same as a forest floor).
A vagrant march time, car
passes silently, arm rests at his side

holding a bell or ground lens
where *c* stands for inessential night –
how that body would
move vs how it actually does –
too abstract &/or not abstract enough

but a closed curve in either case
she might repeat
indicating the shallow eaves
nothing but coats and scarves below the window
his-her face canted to the left

nothing imagined or imaginable
dark and nothing actually begun
so that the color becomes exactly as it was
in the minuscule word for it
scribbled beside an arrow

on the far wall
perfectly how else continuous with memory.
There are pomegranates on the table
though they have been placed there
salt, pepper, books and schedules

all sharing the same error
and measure of inattention.
What she says rolls forward.
I shouted toward motion, other gestured,
child laughs, sky,

traffic, photograph. I
gave real pain, expelled
breath, decided. Both arms in thought,
mirror otherwise, abandoned
structures mostly, the glass

door with its inscription lay open
before us, nothing to fear.

An eye remembers history by the pages of the house in flames, rolls forward like a rose, head to hip, recalling words by their accidents. An ear announces a vertical light without shadow, letters figured across the forehead and wrist, there are no vowels or nouns. Write to me soon I can say nothing more for now. He grew accustomed to the spells of dizziness. I can see about a foot beyond my outstretched arm. I gave up teaching long ago. He expected to die young as if he were immortal. There is a perfect architecture. He grew used to falling unexpectedly. My left eye is closed so I will read these sentences aloud. Mathematics is a minor category of music. The day ends this way each day until it ends. Words listen to the words until you hear them. The words form circles. Water transmits sound. The words cannot be spelled. The table was made of glass which decided to shatter. The dog had an unfortunate habit of farting when important guests were present. They made love by the fire while her husband slept. This mushroom is beautiful and has no name. Lake receives light. By stages you dismember the story. He explained that the word contained a silent *l*. They parted and he entered a cloud. The words do not form circles. I don't think I have a right to leave your letter unanswered. I would like to keep working. I think I see a new way out. The following are matters concerning me and the roof of my mouth. The letters combined into the word for silence. The song came in stanzas as is the manner of such songs. Those who then heard it laughed themselves to death. I was first and last among them. I fled in the direction of the invisible city. I wept before its walls. That night I invented the following dream. It is evening and my father and I are walking east toward Fifth Avenue on the street where we once lived. Every other building has been reduced to rubble as if by an aerial attack. The scene thus resembles those photographs of bombed cities I remember from childhood, except that the buildings remaining appear completely unharmed. Eventually we attempt to enter a favorite restaurant of his but realize that it is in a similar building on a parallel street one block north. We turn away and I wake, as always violently trembling. Once I saw the master of memory sleeping at his desk. Here I will insert the word 'real' to indicate a tree. She brushed against the decanter with her left arm, spilling its contents onto the tile floor. We woke at the same moment and looked up. Here I will insert the word 'red' to indicate a tree. Number imitates measure in a flowered dress. I learned to count to ten and back again. Her fingers sought the indicators at the base of his neck. The words disappeared as he read them. The leaves fell early. Snow caused our arms to fold. Of the seven million one-half have died. Speech seems a welcome impossibility, the room a congeries of useless objects mistaken for events. The song came in fragments as is the nature of such songs. I rose and departed by the far door, no longer able to see. I played among the rats by the river's edge, counted up the condoms and bottles and human limbs, then slept. Wednesday passed in tranquillity. Merchants are building towers, each higher than the last. I shared breakfast with a cat, dinner with an owl. The mountain quivers on the surface of the lake. Your letters reach me at monthly intervals. The angle of the light has changed greatly this past week. I have learned to use my eyes and to distrust them. I am dependent on everything. Words gather into triangles and vertical lines. The sentences they form should not exist. Poems will sometimes overcome them, or else stones.

Symmetrical Poem:
They were afraid of death

He would live against sentences.
They were afraid of death among such trees
formed of empty imaginings
as there are moths we fear
near a hot surface, scales
of the descending song
marked by crucibles and jars
at random intervals. The tiger burns
in this scene or song. It is neither firm
nor a shadow of that moment
washed by early haze
was heard ahead at the gateways
could move them from what they saw.
Something I remember having read
transparency of the mirror
hears him in its turn
hidden where he's never been.
Our guns are there to prove us friendly.
The day's end is soft
as a fold again
and a dog floats headless in the water
careful to avoid the shore.

So the dark figure

So the dark figure falls
backward, arms out and
eyes wide, through the purple

door to another
world. No hint had
been given him

that he would be called
upon and taken
into this painting.

for Bruce McGaw

FIRST FIGURE

Dearest Reader

He painted the mountain over and over again
from his place in the cave, agape
at the light, its absence, the mantled
skull with blue-tinted hollows, wren-
like bird plucking berries from the fire
her hair alight and so on
lemon grass in cafe in clear glass.
Dearest reader there were trees
formed of wire, broad entryways
beneath balconies beneath spires
youthful head come to rest in meadow
beside bend in gravel road, still
body of milky liquid
her hair alight and so on
successive halls, flowered carpets and doors
or the photograph of nothing but pigeons
and grackles by the shadow of a fountain.

Prelude

The limit of the song is this
prelude to a journey to
the outer islands, the generative
sentence, waltz project, forms,
qualities, suns, moons, rings,
an inside-outside then
an outside-inside shaped
with her colored clays. The days
yet propose themselves
as self-evident, everything there
everything here
and you are reading
in a way natural to theatre
a set of instructions
that alters itself automatically
as you proceed west
from death to friendliness, the two
topics upon which you are allowed
to meditate
under the first broad drops
of rain. The planes
will be piloted by ancestors
who have come back to life.
Why the delay.

Lies of the Poem

We welcomed the breeze
could not escape it

The face is turned to an idea
We will never be friends until it's done

His words are over
The false ceiling here

emits a remarkable light
The music is so-so

Were you named for the painting
of the moth of gold

or the stain on the pillow
The face is burned by an idea

cannot escape it
cannot escape or retain it

The body tends to disappear
beneath the wrapping

The ink dries
across a period of years

in which fires occur
at the midpoint between the eyebrows

La-la-la is the germ of sadness
said the speaker in sneakers

Sound decays
and then there is the story

and then the features are erased
The addition of one more chair

and the arrangement is complete
Here another festival

to which no one is invited
and where expectation plays no part

Voice and Address

You are the owner of one complete thought

Its sons and daughters
march toward the capital

There are growing apprehensions to the south

It is ringed about
by enclaves of those who have escaped

You would like to live somewhere else

away from the exaggerated music
in a new, exaggerated shirt

a place where colored stones have no value

This hill is temporary
but convenient for lunch

Does she mean that the afternoon should pass

in such a manner
not exactly rapidly

and with a studied inattention

He has lost his new car
of which you were, once,

a willing prisoner

a blister in your palm
identical with the sky's bowl

reflected in the empty sentence

whose glare we have completely shed
ignoring its freshness

The message has been sent

across the lesser fractures in the glass
where the listeners are expendable

The heart is thus flexible

now straight now slightly bent
and yesterday was the day for watching it

from the shadow of its curious house

Your photo has appeared
an island of calm

in a sea of priapic doubt

You are the keeper of one secret thought
the rose and its thorn no longer stand for

You would like to live somewhere

but this is not permitted
You may not even think of it

lest the thinking appear as words

and the words as things
arriving in competing waves

from the ruins of that place

Lens

I failed to draw a map and you followed it perfectly
because the word for 'cannot' inscribes itself here
to define an atmosphere of absolute trust
which both fastens and unfastens us.

The branches of the pine drooped heavily
in the moist air and this was pleasant
though at times it felt a little unpleasant
that he couldn't balance on his head

where the water trickled down the rocks.
So everything seemed small, even the problem
of whether to buy a new car
or to add a new gadget to the old car

to maintain pride of place on the block. He appears
to have seen the black pubic hair and the vagina
of a woman who squatted there to piss,
the gypsy nurse perhaps

who dealt in magic
holding the infant up with both hands.
The mist would first blur the forest's outline
then half reveal the huge limbs of the trees

or the bedside clock ticking, a red
and a white rose fastened to her breast.
She had sunk into a corner. He told
how gazing at a mountain pool

had once induced a kind of waking sleep
which led to other things.
("I am the lover in the sense of dust"
were his exact words, spoken softly.)

The child was crying out and bleeding.
Indifferently he moved on—the way
did not matter, up or down,
a few steps should be enough.

French for April Fools'

1

I will name it anything I will name you this
and it rains bright stones as you say this

Each of us will call it Egypt
because of the wind

Sarah tripped and fell and spelled nest
and the wind is to blame for this

The wind has gathered a sequence of things as pure facts
Are we to become three as in three less

Is that I or me in a hat
Is that he or she in a word

Is it still early
among such stones

Is it called morning
thus to lie in a slow-drying pool

Once I could not speak of it
Now I am unable to

Truth to tell it was blood spurting from his cock
With her one good eye she would watch

They have lived long enough not to know
What flowers otherwise did we see

These are spirals
though they close at the top

Such answers varied moment by moment
mirroring the weather itself

It is a red landscape
he wondered wonderingly

I find myself here
equivalent to glass

Yet time is to be spent identifying things
This is shouting, this powdered milk

Then it is full of love and will dissolve
Then there are gestures so erected

Then shells or shelves
Then nods or knocks

A statement will be built as if to be said
"Here anything . . ."

It is an architecture
It is a stone step without question

He pulled a gun on the waiter
the young one who had poisoned him

It is a real landscape
they have invented

Truth to tell it was mud
disguised as thoughts to come

Now they are back in the park
the two who have not met before

It is a recent landscape
and the sentence is impossible

Light light murmured the dun horse
from a shaded patch covered with forget-me-nots

It is a questionable first step
impossible to correct

Voice voice cried the dumb horse
The pen trembled and began to write

strange figures on the face of night
Unread they held the answer to our plight

2

Once I could not tell of it
and now I cannot speak at all

So the cloth sticks to you there

A revolution in sportswear has occurred

So it is the park at dusk

Beer is often consumed in the dance world

The woman leans against the table painted yellow

Here it remains cold until morning

In a remote corner I am painting

Another night we slept in a yew tree

The leaf's color results from a disease

(We are speaking of murder not disease)

The bleached shirt waves

I have no crystals for you only a frame

The orange peel, a closed spiral, lies on the plate

It is the park coated with dust

He kept his mistakes beside the bed

His description was careful, even reticent

In a remote corner I am waiting

She removed her clothes as well as herself

He saw inmixing blood

(I is meant by an horizon)

Lightly the choices fell

Here it is a park

3

They have agreed to wait

We had agreed to wait for the rains

They have agreed to wait for the rains to end

I will try the blue mask on

They will remember nothing from before

I will juggle limes from the garden and sing as I'm juggling

The limes will burst where they fall

Their scent will remain after the event is forgotten

Their scent will remain after the room has dissolved

I will recall everything as it was and tell it so

Enough wind or mud to carry us away

Enough lions and monkeys to speak in our place

Enough shadow trains vanishing

Enough soldiers to keep simple order

Enough dead on the sofa enjoying the music

Enough others to serve them with easy grace

Enough *pyramids, heart-swings* and *valid coins of happiness*

Enough *veins full of being*

Enough maternal tones interrupting at night

These tremolos have been substituted for writing

By playing very fast the music remains in place

The fixed arc is designed to erase

What should we do in the coming white days

All those words we once used for things but have now discarded in order to come to know things. There in the mountains I discovered the last tree or the letter A. What it said to me was brief, "I am surrounded by the uselessness of blue falling away on all sides into fields of bitter wormwood, all-heal and centaury. If you crush one of these herbs between your fingers the scent will cling to your hand but its particles will be quite invisible. This is a language you cannot understand." Dismantling the beams of the letter tree I carried them one by one down the slope to our house and added them to the fire. Later over the coals we grilled red mullets flavored with oil, pepper, salt and wild oregano.

The Theory of the Flower

I will read a few of these to see if they exist
(We will translate logos as logos)

He swam in the rock
I am here from a distance

"Now kiss her cunt"
"Now take his cock in your hand"

The film is of a night garden
There is nothing meaningful about the text

There is nothing meaningful about a text
She

brushed away the sand
She brushed away the hand

This is Paradise, an unpunctuated book
and this a sequence of laws

in which the night sky is lost
and the flower of theory is a black spot

upon the foxglove
(These words have all been paid for)

He turns then to shade his eyes from the sun
She edges closer to the fallen log

This is Paradise, a mildewed book
left too long in the house

Now say the words you had meant to
Now say the words such words mean

The car is white but does not run
It fits in a pocket

He slept inside the rock,
a flower that was almost blue

Such is order
which exenterates itself

The islands will be a grave for their children
after they are done

You may use the paper with my name on it
to say whatever you want

I promise not to be so boring next time
never again to laugh and weep so much

which is how spring comes
to the measured center of the eye

The mind is made up
but you forget who it was first spoke

The mind is made up
and then and then

This is the paradise of emptiness
and this the blank picture in a book

I've looked over the photographs and they all are of you
just as we'd been warned

How strange
The winged figure in tuxedo is bending from the waist

The metalion addresses the mirror
and the music of the shattered window

falls unheard past the window below
How strange

but not so strange as speech
mistaken for a book

The phrase "for a moment" is popular in the world
yet not really meant to be said

That is the third or the fourth world
where you can step into a tremor with your tongue

I do not drink of it myself
but intend a different liquid

clear as the glass in which it's held,
the theory of the flower and so on

or the counter-terror of this valley
the fog gradually fills

just as we've been warned
It isn't true but must be believed

and the leaves of the sound of such belief
form a paradise

(pronounced otherwise)
from which we fall toward a window

Idem 1

(for two voices)

Let's see, how could you describe this to a listener? How can I describe this to our listeners? My head is in a steel vise I have been on a long voyage—a sea voyage—I have been travelling, sailing in a white ship, the weather is perfect surface of the water calm I am a woman or man over seven feet tall emerald green in color, malachite blue actually, tourmaline, carnelian, opal, I have been on a long voyage . . .

. . . while I have been open to desire.

Yes, while you have been open to desire, which is also blue.

I have been open to desire . . .

. . . which is like a storm or a small room . . .

. . . while you have been on a voyage, a sea voyage. You spoke of a white ship.

I did?

Yes, a white ship with twin masts. It sat in the water like a smile.

Oh right—like a smile, a white ship, gulls the first sign of land, then driftwood and kelp, then a harbor opens out before us in a perfect half-circle the water like they say clear as glass. She swung to her anchor without a flutter of the sails and was at rest. I have been travelling.

You have been at sea in a white ship with your head in a steel vise.

Exactly correct . . .

. . . while I have been open to desire, my skin an attractive shade of blue, my voice calmly assertive. How can I describe this to a listener. The room is airy and bright, a bit cold in winter, there is a washstand with porcelain pitcher and bowl, a metal cot and a wood-burning stove that rarely works. I have a fine view of the river beyond the terracotta roofs. I assume it's understood that all of this is true.

Exactly correct. And at one point several days that is several minutes ago, didn't you mention a photograph or a painting, something hanging on the wall?

Her red hair, necklace of pearl and green dress.

Necklace of coral.

Necklace of coral, exactly correct . . .

. . . hanging on the wall opposite the bed.

Opposite the bed, yes. How can I describe it to our listeners. She is gazing out of the frame to her right or the viewer's left. Her expression is serious though not severe. What else?

Her arms . . .

. . . her arms hang at her sides. No—her left arm . . . her left arm . . .

She's sitting at a desk.

At her desk, yes, the desk is to the left of the door as you enter and the bed to the right. I'd forgotten the desk, where was I?

In a room overlooking a river and hills beyond covered with olive trees. And I?

On an ocean voyage.

An ocean voyage, yes, I have been travelling, my head in a kind of brace or cage, the surface calm, the light . . .

. . . very flat, so that it seems to open inward, this blueness if I may call it that, buildings empty, hills almost liquid if there *were* hills. You spoke of a white ship, a 'cruising yawl' as I remember.

Yes, I have a description right here:

> "Seen from the air this region of rivers winding their way through flat country presents a pattern of arcs and meanderings of stagnant water. The river-bed itself seems to be edged with pale curves, as if nature had hesitated before giving the river its present, temporary course. At ground level, the Pantanal becomes a dream landscape, where herds of zebus take refuge on the tops of hillocks which look like floating arks, while in the flooded swamps flocks of large birds, such as flamingos, egrets and herons, form dense white-and-pink islands, less feathery however than the fan-like foliage of the caranda palms, the leaves of which secrete a precious wax, and whose scattered clumps offer the only interruption in the deceptively smiling vistas of this aquatic desert."

You mean that's your idea of desire, with all those commas?

We lay becalmed for days, the sea wine-red, my head in a kind of brace or vise. I am a woman or man over seven feet tall, emerald green, crossing an endless field or meadow . . .

. . . hills almost liquid if there *were* hills . . .

. . . and the still air and intense heat of midday . . .

. . . forcing us to take shelter in the shade of the great cottonwoods by the river.

Yes, *perfect,* 'the great cottonwoods by the river.'

And to complete the picture a vast, cobbled public square dating from Roman times, an arcaded town hall decorated with frescoes, and a web of narrow streets filled with couples walking arm in arm. I am sitting in a cafe on the square, my left hand holding a copy of the Kansas City Star folded in half lengthwise, my right holding a spoon and idly stirring coffee in an oversized cup. And so on. The important spot over the head, irregular on one side, straight on the other, like the stripes of the dress, belongs more to her than to the wall; in balancing the head, this vertical form also helps to measure its tilt and the waviness of the hair and costume. On the right shoulder at the sleeve, the odd little puff continues the movement of the hair and accents the inclination of the head. The bands of the dress contribute a soft, wavering current of feeling channeled to the head and prolonged in the silhouette of the hair.

The flame-red hair.

No, dark brown, actually almost black, but I liked that business about the 'smiling vistas of the aquatic desert,' and the 'large flocks of birds.' Thought of using it myself.

Yes, 'the deceptively smiling vistas of this aquatic desert,' and all within the space of a small, sparsely furnished room . . .

. . . overlooking the river. I would usually get up about noon, buy the daily paper and walk to one of the large cafes on the square for coffee and rolls . . .

. . . your face painted blue . . .

. . . and open to desire like a storm or small room, the air always heavy by the river, she raises both arms behind her head to unclasp the coral necklace.

Yes, the sun at its zenith, winged figure with arms extended, and a white ship, exactly correct. Let me tell you what it is you said. The lovers' limbs twist like a river. Their talk is a naming or being named. My back sometimes aches. Their talk hides in the telling. The wind moves us. Wands come and cups, gardens, someone in a cloak, the wind moves us, laws, young girl and the bird at her wrist, colors, bright yellow or blue. I am a woman or man under green sky, garden to my right and then it's the following day. I am a woman or man under emerald sky, wind brushes the river's surface, we talk until our talk becomes hidden.

And when does a play begin?

Don't you remember?

I remember trying to think of who to talk to and what to say. I remember trying to remember what happened on a given day, what word stood for what color, and where we had been and where we had gone. I remember the red studio and the woman in blue, and I remember the one who swallowed his tongue.

Do you remember all the listening?

I remember wandering completely lost and looking for the river. I remember hills and gilded domes . . .

. . . narrow streets between high buildings . . .

. . . narrow streets between high buildings . . .

. . . and the lists of irregular verbs . . .

. . . lists of irregular verbs.

To be is to be seen.

To be is to be seen.

Talk is a naming.

Talk is a naming or a being named . . .

. . . and desire an electric shade of blue . . .

. . . electric shade of blue.

Lovely weather today.

Lovely weather, clear and cold . . .

. . . with emerald sky . . .

. . . under emerald sky, rosemary and hyssop in bloom—uh—in bloom—uh—some marigolds—right, marigolds—clouds—probably clouds—things with—uh—names scattered about—uh—and so on———just 'and so on.'

So *you're* the one who swallowed his tongue!

Now I remember—the play *has* begun!

Idem 2

(for more than two voices)

Rebeginning and beginnings is what she told me or what she showed me, cup raised carefully to lip, *etwas gänzlich neues zu lernen,* cover each page completely and waste no space.

Papa breathes in a great eyeful.

Leaves falling and I can hear each one as it touches the water.

Beginning and rebeginning to fall, and I can hear the water.

(bell rings)

A great eyeful, quiet as a mouse.

A large bucket full of water.

A bucketful and waterfall and a forest.

A voyage.

Seven words learned in winter.

Such as ice to walk on.

Such as Dogtown Common.

(bell rings)

(pitch pipe: slurred F#—F—E, repeated a few times)

F# to E means a winter voyage.

A ship crossing water and a father.

And an icy passage.

But does he have to play while we're trying to talk?

I'm sorry, what?

(pitch pipe: F# with a lot of vibrato, held for a long breath)

A father?

I'm sorry, what?

(pitch pipe: A, with even more exaggerated vibrato, held as long as possible, i.e. until breath is exhausted)

That's better but not . . . but not . . .

(exasperated) . . . but not *what?*

    (bell)

I'm telling you he pissed in his pants when he died.

A great eyeful—something new each time.

I had to clean it all up.

You 'dropped the porcelain cup'?

I had to *clean it all up!*

    (bell)

He tries to breathe his eyes open wide.

A forest calls the boy a child . . .

. . . and breathes a great eyeful . . .

. . . tree and book and book and tree and book . . .

. . . and leaves beginning to fall . . .

. . . and rebeginning to fall . . .

. . . and a sound like water.

Idem 3

(for two voices speaking rapidly and simultaneously)

Tree and book and book and tree and book. Music we refuse to forget. A voyage. A pair of them talk, swallowing hard, then part. She accompanies snow, observes the water in its course, a pair of us talk. She accompanies them both, tries to walk from 'A' to 'B' knee-deep in snow and ends up lost. We listened to music through the winter over there Mozart but over here Corelli and Bach, over there Landini but here Couperin and Rameau. And I talk in my voice because it's warm, because it's warm and faces north. He talks in her voice because he must: Ruby My Dear, Little Rootie Tootie, Pannonica; I Surrender Dear, There's Danger in Your Eyes Cherie, April in Paris; In My Solitude, I'm Getting Sentimental over You, Everything Happens to Me; I Should Care, Remember, Memories of You. He corners her voice in blue light with plain white border, is that you Harry, George I think there's someone at the door, careful with that package Mr. Kupčak it's filled with extremely delicate spiders. New York and London winter and quarter-inch Tuscan winter, faces a lithium blue, eyes never still, pause for breath here then continue at the designated pace. Her voice entered in the shape of a woman's body, music emanating from the left hand, green velvet gown reaching the floor and trailing behind her as she walked. Then another card, dog and wolf baying at the moon, twin towers, the river, and another, Three of Pentacles reversed, mediocrity and weakness, and finally the Six of Swords, a journey by water. Music we remember to forget, and the room itself, bed to the right as you enter, wood-burning stove in far left-hand corner to one side of the window, washstand with mirror and porcelain pitcher and bowl to the other. Thought of it as the language room, entirely nouns, a head-ache that lasted six days, numbness down the left side, lovely curl of smoke. Lights of the fishing boats and of the cars and trucks on the cliff road. Light pouring from the palm of her left hand. He would sit for hours in an apparent daze at one of the tables hidden from the street. Beginnings are what she showed me, scent of thyme and mint in the July air, the Fool a zero holding a white rose. For years he would wake trembling at four in the morning thinking he had heard a scream.

Idem 4

(for one voice)

look I have been had entered a room large or small had entered have been they wondered a door

hills I remember

hills I remember hills white walls at first light lines of red across the snow

look he said I have been

winter like straw bright domes gilded domes narrow halls eight of wands great hope

look she said I am entering

winter a seamless wall winter bent double each word misspoken red dress coral necklace one or two things have been said

and now I say yes

now I say yes to the bridge the dead cross no thicker than a fingernail no wider than a knife eyes fixed on the Gates of Paradise yes to the visible hills the actual hills olive trees with grey underleaf commas between each breath brief tremor smell of gunpowder then screams it was screams and screams all the way through idem the same same hills same trees I remember a door

and one wonders I wondered one wonders what direction and remembers why did they have you ever when he said oh well and remembers was burning with what question what direction oh well had almost I'm turning what star then winter had they been even though falling backward of them would discuss from her dream had been had been worrying isn't yet are coming either hand and remembers oh well oh no don't ever saw nothing fell from means winter fell toward means winter fell into felt nothing is empty she believes me what question then winter had told him we're arriving then opened meaning bridges oh well meaning bridges oh well meaning rivers

and the air perfectly calm sky red yellow or blue streets filled with no one she loved the winter loved to lie for hours in the midnight sun left arm crooked beneath her head the right at her side idem the same is then plus now

so slept through seasons of heat and cold and one of rain fell from a high window she wandered into the hills beyond the river never to be seen again slight rustling of the leaves lilac in flower bed of white poppies he woke inside her dream listen he said how can I said she

as there is no image no city no image no one speaking he would lie the entire day eyes focussed on the ceiling turns toward the wall pen in her left hand small notebook in her right light snow coating the balcony trickle of blood from his thumb sky red yellow or blue grey if rain fell forward bruising her temple cupped palm holding three brilliant stones woke wondering again who she was

and there is as there is no image no city horizon four swords no image a circle tall grass a field from a window river from a field no image no city cold rain seven stars then we slept no image pitched forward toward the water fell over in the doorway light snow against a wall bright stones in her palm no image no city no images to come

Music Rewritten

(after D.S.)

Yes and no then yes and no
Soon there'll be time enough for you

Charlie has swallowed the fluid
L has come inside a box

which some people paid to watch
Yes and no yes and no

You are a damaged set of illustrations
You are a ladder

in a chemical pond
a piece of hurry-up cake

or a true-to-life machine
making a music judged incomplete

by everyone willing to speak
Yes and no and yes and no

In a strange country you feel at home
because the hills there are the opposite of green

exactly as you were told
Now you must go there to prove it's so

Yes and no yes and no
Soon there'll be no time for you

The words are lost in the crease
but order is found at the base of a statue

or better, at the foot of a curved stone wall
in the tangles of the grass

Beneath the shadow of no and yes
nothing can be said

First there's sameness then difference
then the letter X across a face

then a line through a name
which is the wrong name in any case

The Village of Reason

This is a glove
or a book from a book club

This is the sun
or a layer of mud

This is Monday,
this an altered word

This is the village of reason
and this an eye torn out

This is the father
or a number on a chart

This is a substitute,
this the thing you are

This is the varnished picture
or else an accepted response

This is the door
and this the word for door

This is a reflex caused by falling
and this a prisoner with an orange

This is a name you know
and this is the poison to make you well

This is the mechanism
and this the shadow of a bridge

This is a curve
and this its thirst

This is Monday,
this her damaged word

This is the trace
and this the term unmarked

This is the sonnet
and this its burning house

You are in this play
You are its landscape

This is an assumption
the length of an arm

This is a poppy,
this an epilogue

I was talking to the Baroness

I was talking to the Baroness in the Green Room
    The page detached, flew away
toward the northwest
    skimming the still surface
New York was wonderful in those days
    like an island but smaller
though the headlines were awful
    face turned to the wall
the shapes empty colours and forms
    breakwater, mulberry, sign
of the flower opening, sign
    of the flower crystallized
I'm often in London
    less than half alive
Who are the letters A
    Who is Baraka
Sterling Brown in the blue car
    Elmo, Bud, James P.
Nancy and Sluggo
    Axel Hugo Teodor Theorell
to adjust the mirror
    so that the head disappears
who la danseuse magnétique
    qui se mettra d'elle-même en mouvement
sur une table lisse
    Then one must close the mouth quickly
and clench the teeth
    fearing pious old men
all those things that take time
    a maxim handed down to us
between sleeps
    fluid and secret charm
as the z of xylophone
    What fame! What a century

of empty skies, anodynes,
    moving sidewalks
Wet snow is falling once more
    The scene as always is tropical

Sign

Are you asleep M. Valdemar
The survival is untenable
an impossibility of dying
the way smoke rises and comes to rest
overhead, about the light—
that impulse to tell you intimate things
among the floats in a foreign place
projecting oneself into the details
the *a* of anvil for example, anterior,
atopia, at the particular, unstable moment

How install violence, pleasure, irony
and so on as apparent finalities
fragmented into a practice which
erases science, then into words
the opposite of names. So the five
of fingers could become *eyes,*
effort, these, air, dust, where
to another it might mean *flowers,*
a verb whose subject marks years
As for eyes

they are healing, the redness
and pain diminishing each day
Soon the stolen shadow reappears,
the vine on the grey lattice trembles,
the china folk fall from the china wall
An ant is an ideal reader
and there are so many of them
Sad Electra emerges from the forest
and approaches the shore
The conversation, long deferred, begins

easily sometimes, sometimes not at all,
a story whose end I know
and don't know, airs

against the summer's dust
these, head in such an effort
of turning as to resemble
world, "a certain sacrifice"
for the meadow orchids, ospreys,
rugosas and wild currants
Time is passed in saying nothing

by telling things. The chimneys
are not real
but after-images from the dream,
what remained of the houses
in the mountain village
The teacher was the goat-herd's lover
Lightning struck the iron bed,
something to remember in a storm
I do not face the world, I face the wall
Could you be here for that week

Language paralyzes the tongue
and before morning the father is gone
I was born with no right hand
below the street of diamonds
in a city of constant groans
Experience cannot be described
except by us. We
fled down the marble steps
We spoke the prime sentence and dissolved
Everything of smoke was ours

Book of the Yellow Castle

This can be seen as placing a mirror against the page.
The mountain is where we live, a circus there, a triangle
of unequal sides the days no sun appears.

This is life in the square-inch field of the square-foot house,
a September particle, biochip, or liquid in a jar,
and here is snow for the month to follow, light easy to move

but difficult to fix. The cat on the book has fleas.
It's a real cat with real fleas at least,
while the book is neither fixed nor field.

As soon as you had gone an image formed in order to be erased.
First an entryway then a left and right which seemed to be the same.
This letter explains everything and must never be sent.

This other arranges figures along an endless colonnade
imperceptibly darkening toward red. One pretends to be the case
the other is. Mornings the hands tremble, evidence of a missing
    thought.

Arrows will tell you where the words are meant to lead,
from hall to hall apparently. The hair is thinner
and the veins stand out a bit more.

Who could have known he'd be dead within the week,
victim of a loosening thread, the system by which we perceive.
Thus the castle above valley and plain, the logical circuitry and other
    such tricks,

the constant scanning, all kinds of features built in.
And thus the difference between sign and sigh, and the bells which
    signal a return.
The dog instructs the goats, the man instructs the dog.

Should we count the remaining trees to decide what they mean as well,
traces of a conversation possibly, or a larger plan. You enter the stories
    as a surd
and sleep through them, ignoring successive warnings,

shards of cloisonné, broken table legs, a canopied bed.
They are there because the rest have left.
These are scalings of a sentence.

First Figure

The name is spelled without letters how can this be. There are no steps leading to this house, no objects anymore. I have some questions do I not. The reactor has been wounded, that willow perfect, a swimmer not entirely of the world. Humble yourself before the workers. Die eagerly in battle. The water music now unweighted. The terrified child pretends not to hear. Its lions as the library burns. This signals my end. One thing the beloved another the blood. The smoke returns. The hands of the acrobats connect. The name plummets. The eye carves a path. The "A" of "Not A." The attraction to another felt as cork or ink. Calendar etched in wall. The "A" as "Not A." The woman reading, woman sleeping. The view from the studio, Cour de Rohan. The landscape with chestnuts, landscape with goats. The nude resting. The rose of close observation. The smoke as mine returning. The words altered then crossed out. Returning that is into the body. A refusal of the particular body. "I am not somebody here," as spoken by the servant. The medicine on the sill and the light through it. Another light said to be revealing, a third termed awkward. A story in the form of a question to be answered by another in the form of a question and so on. May I speak to Muriel. So much through that door. Myself as Puddin' 'n Pie. The hotel of our crystal delights. Now your turn while the numbers last. Now ours not theirs.

What might be said before the sentences enter: there is no focal point; I have no idea what the future will bring; we did not make the new law ourselves.

The name is felt without letters how can this be. The cat then the ghost of the cat continually reappearing. A reading of an evening. Here the first figure, here the false figure of speech playing with a ring. Here once more the coffee and the moth, damp bread in hunks, habits of afterwards and opposite. There are no steps leading to this. Not ours not theirs. A city of domes soon to be torn down. A sad monkey-house or the five random letters for the fingers of the hand. The story you've been looking for may well lie there. She steps from the shower and reaches for a towel. The story may well lie there in a cloud. Everyone knows these things by heart. Everyone tells these things from the heart.

The word is all that is displaced. This illness I stole from my father. A love of figures, tidiness, fear of error. These are the new remains. She shifted her position almost imperceptibly. He was reluctant to agree at first. They might have it otherwise, simpler perhaps, no columns in the space. They might care to see it in another light, simpler perhaps, deducting shadow. The field itself is yellow, with the usual points of reference. Then evening with its blue coat, perfume jars, obstacles, machines held onto. It was quite a short pleasure. The police know all about it.

for Ben Watkins

This Time

(another for Sarah)

Once I fell in the ocean when
I didn't know I fell in the ocean

Then Momma got me out
This isn't true

only something I remember
Once in the park I broke in half

and lost one half
which half I don't remember

Once I was in a room
It grew larger and larger

why I don't remember
One time I turned blue all over

then got clear as glass
This really happened

but not to me
Once I couldn't see

for a while
so I listened lying down

Another time I looked out the window
and saw myself at the window

across the street
This time it was me

As a Real House

(Sarah's third song)

"I said darkling and you said sparkling"
The play-house appears before us

as a real house in the dark
filled with people cut out

of magazines and postcards
and called real people at the start

Why is the curtain partly drawn
and why does the stair turn

to the left as you climb
and the right going down

Here all day it's midwinter night
and the musicians will continue to play

in the music room
and sleep will never come

This is lesson three
where the fiddler is made real

by the sound she hears
pouring from her fingers

Facades for Norma Cole

These ornaments as we pass
to which thin lines are attached
the straight dark hair, bordered

hollows and lights, double spirals
imagined weights of things
If only I could draw, then

there would be an owl here
a fox in the elm's shadow
Bill do you remember the Chinese man in the stained grey overcoat

lying dead on the snow
by the brick wall
A remarkable document

which must never be published
He turned round to answer
but she was gone

then ran through the streets before passing out
on the steps of a synagogue
the face no longer recognisable

even to my closest friends
These crystals, however
Or put it this way

the particles circle and circle inside the ring
all the while accelerating
until finally by the billions they collide

That's how the missing one was found
Let's call it W for now
which fuels the stars

and so add one more line
extending from the woman with naked breasts
at the center of the arch

to the cat asleep on the child's bed
They spoke of exactly this over coffee
until the glass door shattered

letting the damp wind enter
In her room she showed me
a photograph of her lover

young, heavily muscled and tanned
from several months at sea
We drank wine, smoked

opium through a glass pipe
and climbed to a place on the ridge
a field of nettles and anise

where the remains of the city could be seen
not this city but a previous one
called the pissing rose

or the rhymesters' rose
or the rose of even numbers
or the rose of indecision

or the rose of precise description
or *la rose dialectique, Dominique*
all yours again

in tenuous modes of oscillation
'neath a vestigial sky
"Look—there was a wall here once"

No one did this
It came about by itself
during yesterday's storm

Of this cloth doll which

(Sarah's fourth)

Of this cloth doll which
says Oh yes
and then its face changes
to Once upon a time
to Wooden but alive
to Like the real
to Late into the night
to There lived an old
to Running across ice
(but shadows followed)
to Finally it sneezed
to The boat tipped over
to Flesh and blood
to Out of the whale's mouth

Yes in a circle

(Sarah's fifth)

Yes in a circle the imagined train
word after recent word
you make them up to come to mean
light to shadow day
pond as music's mirror
trees cut from yarrow stalks
would be real in order to seem
a reasonably green place
a reasonable number of roads
some straight, some curved and narrow
beside rails whose perfect parallels
are nowhere else to be seen
but in a sealed and measured space
called here and now for now

SUN

Fifth Prose

Because I'm writing about the snow not the sentence
Because there is a card—a visitor's card—and on that card
       there are words of ours arranged in a row

and on those words we have written house, we have written
       leave this house, we
have written be this house, the spiral of a house, channels
       through this house

and we have written The Provinces and The Reversal and
       something called the Human Poems
though we live in a valley on the Hill of Ghosts

Still for many days the rain will continue to fall
A voice will say Father I am burning

Father I've removed a stone from a wall, erased a picture from
       that wall,
a picture of ships—cloud ships—pressing toward the sea

words only
taken limb by limb apart

Because we are not alive not alone
but ordinary extracts from the tablets

Hassan the Arab and his wife
who did vaulting and balancing

Coleman and Burgess, and Adele Newsome
pitched among the spectators one night

Lizzie Keys
and Fred who fell from the trapeze

into the sawdust
and wasn't hurt at all

and Jacob Hall the rope-dancer
Little Sandy and Sam Sault

Because there is a literal shore, a letter that's blood-red
Because in this dialect the eyes are crossed or quartz

seeing swimmer and seeing rock
statue then shadow

and here in the lake
first a razor then a fact

from Baudelaire Series

A hundred years ago I made a book
and in that book I left a spot
and on that spot I placed a seme

with the mechanism of the larynx
around an inky center
leading backward-forward

into sun-snow
then to frozen sun itself
Threads and nerves have brought us to a house

and clouds called crescent birds are a lifting song
No need to sail further
protesting here and there against some measures

across the years of codes and names
always immortal as long as you remain a man
eating the parts of him indicated by the prophets

stomach skull and gullet
bringing back the lost state
Yes I just dreamed another dream and nobody was in it

Words say, Misspell and misspell your name
Words say, Leave this life

From the singer streams of color
but from you

a room within a smaller room
habits of opposite and alcove

Eros seated on a skull as on a throne
Words say, Timaeus you are time

A page is edging along a string
Never sleep never dream in this place

And altered words say
O is the color of this name

full of broken tones
silences we mean to cross one day

Dear Lexicon, I died in you
as a dragonfly might
or a dragon in a bottle might

Dear Lexia, There is no mind

Dear Book, You were never a book
Panther, You are nothing but a page
torn from a book

Stupid Lake, You were the ruin of a book

Dear Merline, Dearest Lou, Here the streets
have their fullness and their flow
like a blind man on a carousel

Once I was a nice boy
but now I sleep for hours at a time
Snow, You must be my pillow

Dear Merline, Dearest Lou, I see a pheasant on the fence
as I'm writing this
as I see burning Africa by chance
in a cooling wind

Hateful City, In the dream the tree was first a word
then became a column in a dark arcade
What signs for odd and even must be made

Dear George, So long
Will you now have memory again

Who's one and who's nothing
in the game she asked
I couldn't understand the rest

Ideas aren't worth anything
We mirrored each other for an afternoon
The sky is rich with waste
Waiting is the name of this tune
Electrons was a name for this tune

Ideas aren't worth anything
Today space is splendid
The mountains have come loose
Let's unmake something

Ideas aren't worth anything
This is a hazardous bed
called perilous night, some blues
some indigoes, some reds
other colors I forget

Ideas aren't worth anything
This is a trace
to dry in tomorrow's sun

Ideas aren't worth anything
Sometimes (my) blood seems to come in jets
The persons in the poem say this
between liquid spirits and sense
A broken jar says this

I'm writing your letters back to you
which is a sound at least
to mirror another sound
where no other paintings can be found

Imitate me says the elm
Give me an azure sky huge and round
Give me something in words for a change
something that fits on a page
The best paintings are on stone

Ideas aren't worth anything
said a person with two heads
one above and one below
Let's think about this
Let's consider the lace in necklace

or the turquoise on a Turkish door
or the source of each color
at a table by a wall

If we're really mirrors in a poem
what will we call this song
I want to continue on yellow paper
like a person in a room
and like a ladder and like a moth

say the persons of the poem
The tale is told out of school
Your eyes are tired so keep them closed
Once an image broke an arm

A man undergoes pain sitting at a piano
knowing thousands will die while he is playing

He has two thoughts about this
If he should stop they would be free of pain

If he could get the notes right he would be free of pain
In the second case the first thought would be erased

causing pain

It is this instance of playing

he would say to himself
my eyes have grown hollow like yours

my head is enlarged
though empty of thought

Such thoughts destroy music
and this at least is good

You say
A miracle from Heaven

You say
I'm fine I'm fine I'm really going blind

Gay as a skylark today
You say

I haven't an ache or a pain
in me in my body inside

I'm fine I'm fine I'm really going blind
It's a joy to be alive

I had a visitor tonight
with suit and beard and Malacca cane

climbed through my window
and entered me

Is this such a bad thing
Is this a thing at all

Each evening there's a poppy in my brain
which closes before dawn

Whatever happened then will not happen again
Please move my arm

She says, Into the dark—
almost a question—
She says, Don't see things—
this bridge—don't listen

She says, Turn away
Don't turn and return
Count no more lines into the poem
(Or could you possibly not have known

how song broke apart while all the rest watched—
that was years ago)
Don't say things
(You can't say things)

The ground is smooth and rough, dry and wet
Pull the blue coat tighter around you
(There are three parts to you)
I'm not the same anymore

I'm not here where I walk
followed by a messenger confused
(He's forgotten his name)
I'm not here as I walk

not anyone on this path
but a figure of walking
a figure projected exactly this far
followed by the messenger confused

(He's forgotten his name)
Don't say his name for him
Don't listen to things
(You can't listen to things)

Some stories unthread what there was
Don't look through an eye
thinking to be seen
Take nothing as yours

after Rilke, "Orpheus. Eurydike. Hermes"

A word is coming up on the screen, give me a moment. In the meantime let me tell you a little something about myself. I was born in Passaic in a small box flying over Dresden one night, lovely figurines. Things mushroomed after that. My cat has twelve toes, like poets in Boston. Upon the microwave she sits, hairless. The children they say, you are no father but a frame, waiting for a painting. Like, who dreamed you up? Like, gag me with a spoon. Snow falls—winter. Things are aglow. One hobby is Southeast Asia, nature another. As a child I slept beneath the bed, fists balled. A face appeared at the window, then another, the same face. We skated and dropped, covering our heads as instructed. Then the music began again, its certainty intact. The true dancers floated past. They are alive to this day, as disappearing ink. After the storm we measured the shore. I grew to four feet then three. I drove a nail through the page and awoke smiling. That was my first smile. In a haze we awaited the next. You said, "Interior colors." You said, "Antinucleons." You said, "Do not steal my words for your work." Snow falls—winter. She hands out photographs of the Union dead. Things are aglow. I traded a name for what followed it. This was useless. The palace of our house has its columns, its palms. A skull in a handcart. I removed a tongue and an arm, but this was useless. On Tuesday Freud told me, "I believe in beards and women with long hair. Do not fall in love." Is there discourse in the tropics? Does the central motif stand out clearly enough? In this name no letters repeat, so it cannot be fixed. Because it's evening I remember memory now. Your English I do not speak. A word is coming up on the screen.

I have answers to all of your questions. My name is the word for wall, my head is buried in that wall. When I leap over that wall I think of my head, I can assure you. And into the garden: paradise—broken bottles, tractor tires, shattered adjectives (fragments of a wall). The sky beyond on fire, this is true. The hills beyond a glinting gold, also true. And you married to that clown, that ape, that gribbling assassin of light. Your daughters will avenge you. And into the garden: paradise—the soldiers, their rifles, their boots, their eyes narrowed, searching for a lost head. Or a stolen head? The head of a pornographer. There, I've said it. Pink nipples grow hard as she brushes them with her lips. Moans can be heard coming from poems—poems you, Senator, want desperately to read but will not let yourself, since you are a citizen, proud and erect. And out of the head laughter, tears, tiny bubbles of spit. It is a head from another century, the last one or the next.

for C. E.

Barely anything to say, everything said. But you break, as a hooded traveller, scattering images across the plain, I among them and other I's. This prose, a

color sampler, is meant for you: *Voile bleu, Dame du Sud, Bleu Medicis,* fifty dead on the tarmac, creases of the hand. Is there still an outside, uncancelled as yet by other

codes appearing in service to what

revolutionary pleasures, what floods
of a matrix in slow dissolve

there on the screen, where everything is named difference, and is always the same for that reason, since you've watched it many times before and counted the limbs?

Glides and rests.

Let's say a particular music, in profile.

Let's say mythological figures, freeze dried, who—once immersed— emerge from their gelatin capsules: Syrinx, Polyeidos, the Dioskuroi; Earth Diver, Frog and Moon, Mephisto.

They refuse you their stories, pour soot on you
                                     and into you.

And that other music, sort of gasped out now by the synthetron, the instruments slightly more than real, if ontically problematic at best.

Or we might say just as you said, It's snowing in Paris, which does not exist.

(A painting of that.)

Or the problem we began with, that words have no letters.

And that each of those letters has a distinctive shape. Or shade. Impossible to remember.

Desire was a quotation from someone.

Someone says, This This. Someone says, Is.

The tribe confronts a landscape of ice.

He says, I will see you in the parallel life.

She says, A miser has died from the cold; he spoke all his sentences and meant no harm.

My voice is clipped, yours a pattern of dots.

Three unmailed have preceded this, a kind of illness.

Now I give you these lines without any marks, not even a breeze

dumb words mangled by use

like reciting a lesson or the Lord's Prayer.

How lovely the unspeakable must be. You have only to say it and it tells a story.

A few dead and a few missing

and the tribe to show you its tongue. It has only one.

I am an architect in Vienna
dead and a writer
in a blood red bed

I eat with a fork the meat, the violin

I've let go my practice of this violin

In Vienna there are no musicians

Is my violin broken again
I asked at age 9. 10

So then I sat down and was going to get rid of this violin

I can't play it for beans anyway

I'm an architect in a town of architects

No buildings

All my brother architects are dead
or else asleep with their sisters in bed

Call me Eric
whose grandfather mended the violin

whose mother once taught him to hate the violin
and play dead

I've designed a circle and a bridge

My tears are for the person I miss, the down on her lip

                                        to Jandl

We will call today
In Search of a Newt,

a language that is ordinary, the same
as language only smaller. The ship

did land, Michael, and the natives
did speak, so we killed them.

Souviens-toi? All things were as one
then, behind the electronic fence.

In tongues books were written, suns
rose wherever we placed them

and lawnchairs and trees too
were painted in. The Gasthaus

was Eros itself, with that ghost
of the dancer hovering about.

The more-than-grass
stretched toward the sea.

We floated
and it could be said that we floated.

upon rewitnessing "The Landing of Rochambeau"

Sun

A headless man walks, lives
for four hours

devours himself
You bring death into your mouth—X

we are called—
sleep, festinate, haul rocks

The eye follows itself across the screen
Words pass backward

onto the tongue
are swallows

in clay cliffs
The sea's no picture at all

blue mountain incised with a face
ends in burnt cluster

mud, private telematics, each
person controlling a machine

This is owned by the Man Roy works for
in Insurance work

Words will say this
resolved to write a play

Place an allogene within the graft
The hood is black with two holes for my mouths

I am not the prisoner
of such a space

In a certain way all this still exists
but the scene and the mirror no longer exist

. . . sky a painter's house
No yes

You churn hymns into fragments
No then yes

Asleep you set fire to this house

Mr. Duck and Mr. Mouse
mass as shadows

An indefinite calculus
watches, writes and rewrites

Animals are emperors, tamed and fabulous

The world is an object

The world is an object

Place yourself here as if on a surface

Replace horizon with an equals sign

B says, It could be made of silk,
of marble, of extract of clouds

B asks, Is the discourse
of objects specific

Can one imagine laws . . .
Can you decode the birth of the sign

from the miniskirt, the unconscious, TV, the
mirage

of the referent, the equation
of A with A

A body disappears into itself
its mirror self or sister self

The marks have no dimension
They stream from the creases of the hand

Let's call this The Quiet City
where screams are felt as waves

plunging or released, a content
and an alibi, a matrix

at zero stains you with ink
My speech explaining the layers went very well

B says, The blind are hideous, the city laughs
and you tread on corpses in your mask

Says that winter nights it's both sweet and sad
to hear a bell

Says that these lines
have neither eyes nor ears

and that once you woke entangled in her hair

Mr. Tulliver assaults his horse, wants his money

Chainsaw memories cause laughter among the hierophants
She spread her legs wide and braced them

We, the center, offer narratives
We have three days to live

in smog, crossing the Plains of Id
On the wall it is written:

Symbolism died for your sins
Own the body you desire

This I is the I who speaks
(signed Scardanelli)

Day One is called Tongues

Day Two might be This-and-Only-This

Day Three is Antinomy

It was nice to come back here
lots of mountains, etc,
living pillars of flesh

Day One is called Trace

Day Two is Map

Day Three is X, Name of X, Name of N

It is a spring day in a state of siege

I offer you a flat land

Sun flares, then divides

From the Côte des Morts she writes,
The town has changed and artists are objects

and objects have no skin—
I could not have returned

To the left of the piano is theory

Call it Alpha in Lyre
Call it Ceterae or Last Nights,

The Blue Guide, Grid, The Private
Experience of the Blinking Man

Call it Ones (split open)
Call it A Scratch Band from Duluth

written entirely inside
the body of another

its moments free of him
The pages turn themselves

Then I knead my breasts so that milk spurts out
across his face and neck, silver

coin under the tongue, bread and money
for the ferryman. This wire

travels through her teeth
as if through a slot

I ate all the food in the world
and left people hungry

All these stories are the same
There is only one story—

but not really—
so I swallowed the corn and all was well

For three-hundred years they let me eat undisturbed
Now there is a present of watery light

cast onto you, the body bent back
in an attitude of reception

A statue controls our weather
Call it Live at the It Club

someone falling or depicted as falling
mirror folded about you and within you

unreadable, even invisible
The snow is ours, no part of this page

coating Moscow's courtyards

Call it Hilbert's Dream or Papyrology,
Simulations or The Bathers

I nudged Dante off my desk
into the flood. The others quickly followed

streaming from that cafe
once known as The Rose

We spoke in the zero code
system of assemblage and separation

arcuate scar, shadow and necklace
doubled by their reflections

then redoubled in the lens
34,000 words spread out before me

words like incarnadine, tide and cheer
asymptote, locus, tear or tear

waiting to say things
(you cannot say things)

and the anagram for *names,*
for *stone,* for *arm*

claustral body woven from signs
Call it Table or call it Trace

B says, The real table does not exist
I sang my name and turned into a skeleton

in a tree, you below me
I'm writing this diary in the cold

of our winter here
the city like a fortress

Toller has betrayed the Revolution
The clock is set

                    Our pages

burn themselves

as theater

                    awaiting an extinguishing
mist

I sang my name but it sounded strange
I sang the trace then

without a sound,
then erased it

The body of a cellist is floating in the sea

Let us number all the sentences beginning with one
then one plus one. Here

light offers its signal, its parts
Words pop out of a rock

It is the last book, a point
before the next. A body

has been sighted floating in the sea
At center stage she bows

then the dancers surround her
Malcolm sat beside me

He spoke quietly
about music

This notebook contains shadows
nothing else. Dystopic

figures confound the matrix
bore holes in it

through us. One speaks
and the other doesn't

I say space to mean
an ache or a page

twinned logics of a face
The remains

of a fly in a bottle
seek our gaze

We have invented a mechanism for preserving the dead
Here only the head is shown
as encased within a block of glass

The head read us this:
You have one eye too many; masked

as myself you speak;
suspend thought from its bolt

The head told them this:
I want the stolen word here,

statue fallen silently among the leaves
where we've come to sleep;

a screen is ours,
it's called Ways and Means,

its name is The old, old man,
and its name is called Haddock's eye

The head read us this:
I have water

I have bone
Everything's a sign

to a talking stone
A thread read us this

Here whispers collect dust;
fields fold up then out;

enter through the curtain
and swallow your words;

a screen is ours
infinite, hyaline

a woman bent double in the street
is screaming Money Money

The throat read us this

I was sitting in the dark ivy at the gate
of the desiring-machine no windshield no

wheels I was sitting in the forest the great
counter-weight I was truly lost I was seated

behind a screen I was aware of things those
things were me amazing the forked branch

spilling names I had been-not I
had been not-lost I had seen you once

and clearly once I had been remembered
only once the boy

shouts Mica and gleams I am in a
versionary state you are in

me as history I fix
and crystal to it

inside the inside once

                    alp air

                    down the lane

I travelled a little

was limned

where some father says
Your words are not connect

The path we take is 1 to 6
ending in a bubble. Does all

music enter into these cries

Do stones explode at dusk
in us

Did you paint on the walls
of the deaf man's house

I travelled a little

to the snow-fields, then down

How to say I or
we in rival voice

These
new waves circused in a void

placed themselves before us
spoke their tactics

and their practices, traced
each friction and line

each seam of an increasingly minuscule night

A house you enter and remark
I no longer understand
what such things are for

Name you this: a region,
a language, a pot of stew

A magical chain
shreds particles and objects

Name you this: painter
of only shadows, paramorph,

figure walking
in ice, erased figure falling

whose liquid we will drink
as it coats our skins

Story of hands abandoning their fingers,
of an organ emerging from the throat

A man with dynamite strapped to his waist
sings for the first time

        lens
     question

                           in

And black
As when

Story of golden doves with silver dots,
a word beside itself

This building is not

A word is beside itself

A word twists backward
peeling its skin up over its face

A word looks behind itself
Here you are law, a boat

in flames or a gaze
Does it say book

anywhere on this book
Does it say Jonah in this book

Does it say screen or stain
and compose a tone of light

directly behind the eye
Suppose there's a portrait

on this paper I'm holding
Day and night

the shattered statuary was heaping up
before the one newly named

La Violaine or The Park
Call you this with a dot

Time of signal fires, no
memory or map. The

inframaculit wakes
at the sound of breaking glass

Throughout the city
there's the sound of breaking glass

We have forgotten it
slipped between the pages

falls outside
what is thought

After the angled dark
what is meant by book

Scribed on the streaming body:
Song to End a World

Through the glass box words
pass unrecognised, thinking us

now dead to you, reader,
now an ammonite curve

incomplete, now tablet
of faint scratches, now redness

in margins, now past
and pastness. Now a filament of light

penetrates the image-base
where first glyphs are stored,

Lucy and Ethel, the Kingfish,
Beaver and Pinky Lee

are spoken, die and undie
for you

like a war viewed from poolside
by philosophers and sheiks,

senators and dialectician-priests
The day has begun

The bed aches in its dream
of durable densities, rain,

a house whose balconies
vibrate and hum

in space. Do not write
in this space. Never sleep

in this house. At the Salle Waag
we spoke in growls

while at the Meise and Kaufleuten
there were final afterwords

and many teeth fell out
among the many mirrors and many lamps

hurled to the ground
This is not The Shining Windows

nor a glance
at "the sea"

Once your name was Therefore
then Rubble then Ash

question of whose body
in what photograph

I do not recognise this music
Moon drops from sky and burns in field;

man hangs from rope; woman points gun
toward a world where

I is a person
formed of letters in salt,

Five Figures in a Room
or The Triadic Ballet

The clock is set for "departure"

Rowers curl through this air
bent against it, spewing sand,

light-lines and ochre points,
songs in the future-past

will have been known as
The Well, The Needle's Eye

and The Book of the Machines
The branch bleeds

so that a soul can speak
twilight disk

writ on you
ilynx and alea

desire in a net
A new year

is being recorded here,
long saplings with paper blossoms

hollyhocks and painted sleds
Everything is number

a street and the figures on it
stolen genres and formats

in a bar in Bangkok
waiting for death above the flames

(You are coated with fourteen microns of gold
so whatever you say is true)

———

because the words disgusted me why write?
signed Schelling, signed An Arm or A Door, signed The Desert
        to the West

———

This is how one pictures the Angel of History
signed Series B, signed A or letter of A, signed Bakhtin's Names

———

This isn't time so I'll leave you now
signed It, signed Mantis, signed A Stone in the Grass

———

I lost my brain when I put a fork through my hat
signed House of Music

———

This was the trouble with the sun-dial or saint dial
signed Writing Itself

———

The lines through these words
form other, still longer lines

dust in a steady shower
It is our fortune to have been born

at the crossroads of a chiasma
in a land known as How to Laugh

and How to Die. Did spine write this

          story of

my life in a pyramid
designing those pyramids yet to come

those galaxies now being formed,
constellations, touching myself, rubbing against different objects

in total darkness
a year of extreme pain

but fortunately I am perfectly dead
and can see into the past through a lens

signed The World As It Is
tango converted to a fugue

black milk, golden hair
cliffs, bridges, grey lake

and a grave in the air
It rains

It burns
Carry something to somewhere

Tie something to something else
Hold your head in your right hand

as a lantern
a light impossible for this season

and so we turn away from these sounds
raise our Illyrian hats

visit our beds
and ring a bell

X, name of X
we are

A bark sets out on the honeycomb's flow
We called it Le Départ

Sun

Write this. We have burned all their villages

Write this. We have burned all the villages and the people in them

Write this. We have adopted their customs and their manner of dress

Write this. A word may be shaped like a bed, a basket of tears or an X

In the notebook it says, It is the time of mutations, laughter at jokes, secrets beyond the boundaries of speech

I now turn to my use of suffixes and punctuation, closing Mr. Circle with a single stroke, tearing the canvas from its wall, joined to her, experiencing the same thoughts at the same moment, inscribing them on a loquat leaf

Write this. We have begun to have bodies, a now here and a now gone, a past long ago and one still to come

Let go of me for I have died and am in a novel and was a lyric poet, certainly, who attracted crowds to mountaintops. For a nickel I will appear from this box. For a dollar I will have text with you and answer three questions

First question. We entered the forest, followed its winding paths, and emerged blind

Second question. My townhouse, of the Jugendstil, lies by Darmstadt

Third question. He knows he will wake from this dream, conducted in the mother-tongue

Third question. He knows his breathing organs are manipulated by God, so that he is compelled to scream

Third question. I will converse with no one on those days of the week which end in *y*

Write this. There is pleasure and pain and there are marks and signs. A word may be shaped like a fig or a pig, an effigy or an egg
                                                                but
there is only time for fasting and desire, device and design, there is only time to swerve without limbs, organs or face into a
                                                        scientific
silence, pinhole of light

Say this. I was born on an island among the dead. I learned language on this island but did not speak on this island. I am writing to you from this island. I am writing to the dancers from this island. The writers do not dance on this island

Say this. There is a sentence in my mouth, there is a chariot in my mouth. There is a ladder. There is a lamp whose light fills empty space and a space which swallows light

A word is beside itself. Here the poem is called What Speaking Means to Say
        though I have no memory of my name

Here the poem is called Theory of the Real, its name is Let's Call This, and its name is called A Wooden Stick. It goes yes-yes, no-no. It goes one and one

I have been writing a book, not in my native language, about violins and smoke, lines and dots, free to speak and become the things we speak, pages which sit up, look around and row resolutely toward the setting sun

Pages torn from their spines and added to the pyre, so that they will resemble thought

Pages which accept no ink

Pages we've never seen—first called Narrow Street, then Half a Fragment, Plain of Jars or Plain of Reeds, taking each syllable into her mouth, shifting position and passing it to him

Let me say this. Neak Luong is a blur. It is Tuesday in the hardwood forest. I am a visitor here, with a notebook

The notebook lists My New Words and Flag above White. It claims to have no inside
   only characters like A-against-Herself, B, C, L and
N, Sam, Hans Magnus, T. Sphere, all speaking in the dark with their hands
   G for Gramsci or Goebbels, blue hills, cities, cities with hills, modern and at the edge of time

F for alphabet, Z for A, an H in an
arbor, shadow, silent wreckage, W or M among stars

What last. Lapwing. Tesseract. X perhaps for X. The villages are known as
These Letters—humid, sunless. The writing occurs on their walls

AT PASSAGES

Letters to Zanzotto

Letter 1

Wasn't it done then undone, by
us and to us, enveloped, sid-
erated in a starship, listing
with liquids, helpless letters—
what else—pouring from that box,
little gaps, rattles and slants

Like mountains, pretty much worn down
Another sigh of breakage, wintering
lights, towers and a century of hair,
cloth in heaps or mounds, and limbs,
real and artificial, to sift among

Did they really run out of things
or was it only the names for things
in that radial sublimity, that
daubed whiteness, final
cleansing and kindness, perfect
snow or perfection of snow

leaving us peering at the bridge,
its central syllable missing,
and the ground here and there
casually rent, cartoon-like,
lividly living, calling in counter-talk:

Whoever has not choked on a word

But Dr. Sleep and his Window of Time?
Pallas and Vesta? Antibodies in plants?
Torches, cobbles and red flags?
The calcined walls facing whenness
meant as witness. The few
trans things smelling of sex and pine

said what to them
and to us as them

Letter 2

Belowabove: hum of the possible-to-say?

Forest in which the trees grow downward
and through the leaves and mist a small boat in flames?

Song of the closed mouth?
Of an alphabet underground?

Letter 3

Our errors at zero: milk for mist, grin
for limbs, mouths for names—or else hours

of barks, stammers and vanishings, nods
along a path of dissolving ice. The sign

we make for "same as"
before whatever steps and walls,

shutters flapping in the lighted body
called null or called vocative. I'd wanted to ask

about dews, habits of poplar, carousel,
dreamless wealth, nets, embers

and folds, the sailing ship "Desire"
with its racks and bars

just now setting out. This
question to spell itself. And the waves of us

following what follows,
retelling ourselves

what we say we've said
in this tongue which will pass

Letter 4

Almost or *more than* or *almost alive*

But the body of another you attempt to lift,
the body you try to address
and the doubtful or the dark
of this sudden, stripped
winter and its winds?

A train housed in glass?

And the "supplement of sun"?

But the body you enter
with your tongue, with
the words on its tip,
words for chemicals and tastes
and almost remembered names,

hurriedly chalked equations
for the kinds of snow in our time
and always, behind

the landscape,
a snow more red than white?

Letter 5

Desired, the snow falls upward,
the perfect future, a text
of wheels. You were born here
between noise and anti-noise
in first bits of film,

silvers of image, the *of*
and its parts—particle
as wave—the perfect
future's steps, its thousand lakes
bells, remarks, lunations and dismays

Days were called the speed book
then the scream book, rail
book then the book of rust, perfect-
bound, perfect shadow of a clock
the photophilographer assembles in negative,

negative sun or negative shade,
negative dust pulled from the ground
and the images negated in ornate frames,
firebricks, funnels and trucks,
figment and testament as one

Letter 6

Dear Z,
So we accused mimesis, accused

anemone
and the plasma of mud,

accused pleasure, sun
and the circle of shadow

Letter 7

But the buried walls and our mouths of fragments,
no us but the snow staring at us . . .

And you Mr. Ground-of-What, Mr. Text, Mr. Is-Was,
can you calculate the ratio between wire and window,

between tone and row, copula and carnival
and can you reassemble light from the future-past

in its parabolic nest
or recite an entire winter's words,

its liberties and pseudo-elegies,
the shell of a street-car in mid-turn

or scattered fires in the great hall
I would say not-I here I'd say *The Book of Knots*

I'd say undertows and currents and waterspouts,
streaks of phosphorous and riverine winds

Dear Z, I'd say it's time, it's nearly time, it's almost, it's
        just about, it's long
past time now time now for the vex- for the vox- for the
        voices of shadows,

time for the prism letters, trinkets and shrouds,
for a whirl in gauzy scarves around the wrecked piazza

Messieurs-Dames, Meine Herren und Damen, our word-balloon,
        you will note, is slowly
rising over the parched city,

its catacombs, hospitals and experimental gardens,
its toll-gates, ghettos and ring-roads,

narcoleptics and therapists and stray cats
Ladies and Gentlemen, our menu for this flight,

due to temporary shortages,
will be alpha-omega soup, Bactrian hump, and nun's farts

As we enter the seventh sphere, you will discover a thin
layer of ice just beginning

to form on your limbs
Do not be alarmed, this is normal

You will experience difficulty breathing, this is normal
The breathing you experience is difficulty, this is normal

Dear Z, Should I say space
constructed of echoes, rifts, mirrors, a strange

year for touring the interior
Should I say *double dance, Horn, axis* and *wheel*

Dear A, Scuttled ships are clogging the harbors
and their cargoes lie rotting on the piers

Prepare executions and transfusions
Put on your latest gear

Letter 8

(cirrostratus)

So *A*'s finally, alephs and arcades,
the bone-dice thrown

beside the chained gates
And the cawing of out-there: bells, charged hearts, old films

threaded past narrative's lip
But what does the whir- the wer- what does the word

need—world need to be gone—to perform—what
does the world

before you need
to become perfect

They are swimming below the cliff-heads and the wind
Brickworld, chimneys, when-if-not-

When-if-not-when, foam
and wrack, wheeling of terns

And aloud, unearthed
as a language of nets

Actual blue and citron
Actual grey underleaf—so

many bundles to burn—take them to the woods
and burn them in heaps

A's before B's
Take the versions in your mouth

Take inside into your mouth
unearthed, all smoke, blue

and citron, actual word
for that earth and that smoke

Seven Poems Within a Matrix for War

H

We sat on the cliff-head
before twin suns.

For all I know we were singing
"Dancing on the Ceiling."

Descending I became lost
but this is nothing new.

From the screen poured
images toward me.

The images effected a hole
in the approximate center of my body.

I experienced no discomfort
to my somewhat surprise.

This was many weeks ago
many times of days ago.

Yet as far as history goes
it was no time at all.

Many kinds of days ago
I should have said above.

The body has altered
many times since.

Has bent a little over on its stem
and shed a layer of film.

Winter has come and gone
should be remembered.

White occasions like clouds
she may once have whispered.

To that I would add, fields
unplanted, some still burning.

Wonderless things
days at a time.

As a storm begins as a night storm
to end as an ice storm.

Some by now certainly have left
to seek shelter in the mountains.

Only to be met there
by the force of spring rains.

Paths turned to mud
boulders torn loose from above.

The difficulties with burying the dead
she may then have said.

But this letter is something like a door
even if a false door.

Unvoiced as breath
voiced as ash.

To that I would add
there is a song opposite itself.

To that I would add, we have drawn
necessary figures from the sack of runes or tunes.

Echo and wormwood
conspire at the base of the throat.

Snail climbing acanthus
measures our pace.

On the plate by the mark of difference
a mark is made we call the first mark.

Weathering so
the wheel of days.

Gaia the bag lady
in sadness below.

Construction of the Museum

In the hole we found beside the road
something would eventually go

Names we saw spelled backward there

In the sand we found a tablet

In the hole caused by bombs
which are smart we might find a hand

It is the writing hand
hand which dreams a hole

to the left and the right of each hand

The hand is called day-inside-night
because of the colored fragments which it holds

We never say the word desert
nor does the sand pass through the fingers

of this hand we forget
is ours

We might say, Memory has made its selection,
and think of the body now as an altered body

framed by flaming wells or walls

What a noise the words make
writing themselves

for E.H.
11 apr 91

Untitled (April '91)

La narrativa says you must paint a flower
paint a flower with a death's head

flower with a death's head at its center
center with a desert at its center

clock with ochre hands
its face a sun the sun

a multiple sun at 3 a.m.
sun of limbs and sun of the lens

flower as if it were a limb
anemone, rose, yellow marigold

gravity a word from the narrative
word that bends in the narrative

as if suns would flower as sparks of paint
then fall before the retinal net

fall into actual space
space of minarets and streets

Says, Here is a word you must erase
a word made of particles of paint

Here is a word with no points in space
The Higgins black ink has dried in its bottles

so it's true, as angels have said
that there are things of glass

light-gatherers, cat's-eyes, keys and bells
and that glass is a state of sand

It's impossible to hold such a key in your hand
and it's light you see traveling through angels of glass—

through knells—
causing the il- lis- les- the li- lil- lit-

forming the l's you're never to understand
like the tongues of syllables wreathed in the wells,

like tongue-tied and transparent angels
The painting wall still stands

Studio at night
Everything in place

to P.G.

H

Yet the after is still a storm
as witness bent shadbush
and cord grass in stillness

sand littered with the smallest of fragments
whether shell or bone
That city we are far from

is still frozen, still in ruins
(except its symmetries be renewed
by sleep, its slant colors redeemed)

Nothing has changed but its name
and the air that it breathes
There's still no truth in making sense

while the ash settles, so fine that
planes keep falling from the sky
And the name once again to be the old one

Saint Something, Saint Gesture, Saint Entirely the Same
as if nothing or no one had been nameless in the interim
or as if *still* could be placed beside *storm*

that simply, as in a poem
Have you heard the angels with sexed tongues,
met the blind boy who could see with his skin,

his body curled inward like a phrase,
like an after in stillness or a letter erased
Have you seen what's written on him

as question to an answer or calendar out of phase
Add up the number of such days
Add *illness* and *lilt* as formed on the tongue

Add that scene identical with its negative,
that sentence which refuses to speak,
present which cannot be found

Wheel

You can say the broken word but cannot speak
for it, can name a precise and particular shade
of blue if you can remember its name
(Woman of the South, New Lilac, Second Sky?)

As the light, close to blinding, fell—falls
in bars across a particular page, this
then another, some other
followed far too closely by night

Or as the sleeping
pages recall themselves, one by one,
in dream-riddled, guarded tones,
recall themselves from path

to sloped meadow, meadow
to burnt shore, shore
to poised wave, dismay
to present, any present

of the bewildered and the buried alive
(we've been told they were buried alive)
Is there a door he hasn't noticed
and beyond it a letter which created the door

or claims it created a door
which would open either way

Twenty-four Logics in Memory of Lee Hickman

The bend in the river followed us for days
and above us the sun
doubled and redoubled its claims

Now we are in a house
with forty-four walls
and nothing but doors

Outside the trees, chokecherries, mulberries and oaks
are cracking like limbs
We can do nothing but listen

or so someone claims,
the Ice Man perhaps, all enclosed in ice
though the light has been shortening our days

and coloring nights the yellow of hay,
scarlet of trillium, blue of block ice
Words appear, the texture of ice,

with messages etched on their shells:
Minna 1892, Big Max and Little Sarah,
This hour ago

everyone watched as the statues fell
Enough of such phrases and we'll have a book
Enough of such books

and we'll have mountains of ice
enough to balance our days with nights
enough at last to close our eyes

"or anything resembling it"

The hills like burnt pages
Where does this door lead

Like burnt pages
Then we fall into something still called the sea

A mirrored door
And the hills covered with burnt pages

With words burned into the pages
The trees like musical instruments attempt to read

Here between idea and object
Otherwise a clear even completely clear winter day

Sometimes the least memorable lines will ring in your ears
The disappearing pages

Our bodies twisted into unnatural shapes
To exact maximum pleasure

From the view of what is in any case long gone and never was
A war might be playing itself out beyond the horizon

An argument over the future-past enacted in the present
Which is an invisible present

Neva streaming by outside the casement
Piazza resculpted with bricolage

Which way will the tanks turn their guns
You ask a woman with whom you hope to make love

In this very apartment
Should time allow

What I would describe as a dark blue dress with silver threads
And an overturned lamp in the form of a swan

A cluster of birches represents negativity
Flakes of ash continue to descend

We offer a city with its name crossed out
To those who say we are burning the pages

from Untitled

Eighth Sky

It is scribbled along the body
Impossible even to say a word

An alphabet has been stored beneath the ground
It is a practice alphabet, work of the hand

Yet not, not marks inside a box
For example, this is a mirror box

Spinoza designed such a box
and called it the Eighth Sky

called it the Nevercadabra House
as a joke

Yet not, not so much a joke
not Notes for Electronic Harp

on a day free of sounds
(but I meant to write "clouds")

At night these same boulevards fill with snow
Lancers and dancers pass a poisoned syringe,

as you wrote, writing of death in the snow,
Patroclus and a Pharaoh on Rue Ravignan

It is scribbled across each body
Impossible even to name a word

Look, you would say, how the sky falls
at first gently, then not at all

Two chemicals within the firefly are the cause,
twin ships, twin nemeses

preparing to metamorphose
into an alphabet in stone

St.-Benoît-sur-Loire
to Max Jacob

Recursus

The voice, because of its austerity, will often cause dust to rise.

The voice, because of its austerity, will sometimes attempt the representation of dust.

Someone will say, I can't breathe—as if choking on dust.

The voice ages with the body.

It will say, I was shaped by light escaping from a keyhole.

Or, I am the shape of that light.

It will say, For the body to breathe, a layer must be peeled away.

It will say, What follows is a picture of how things are for me now.

It will say, The rose is red, twice two is four—as if another were present.

The dust rises in spirals.

It will say, The distance from Cairo to anywhere is not that great.

As if one had altered the adjustment of a microscope.

Or examined its working parts.

Possibly an instrument covered with dust and forgotten on a shelf.

Beside a hatbox and a pair of weathered boots.

The voice will expand to fill a given space.

As if to say, This space is not immeasurable.

This space is not immeasurable.

When held before your eyes.

And which voice is it says (or claims to say), Last night I dreamt of walls and courses of brick, last night I dreamt of limbs.

As you dream—always unwillingly—of a writing not visible and voices muffled by walls.

As if the question: lovers, prisoners, visitors.

The voice, as an act of discipline or play, will imitate other voices.

This is what I am doing now.

This is what I'm doing now.

The clock behind my back, its Fusée mechanism.

Voice one recognizes from years before.

Beneath water, hidden by a spark.

Here at the heart of winter, or let's say spring.

Voice with a history before its eyes.

With a blue dot before its eyes.

History of dust before its eyes.

It will say, as if remembering, The letter S stands for a slow match burning.

On the table before me.

No numbers on this watch.

And I live in a red house that once was brown.

A paper house, sort of falling down.

Such is the history of this house.

It looks like this.

Looks just like this.

We think to say in some language.

to Porta

Erolog

(a reply)

Asked, Don't you dream, do you ever
or once, did you once—the white

(he)—the white
rain, railings, head-high, erased, no

shadow. And our menhirs, watch-
towers, carbon shores, our almosts—

of speaking, or speaking-seeing, her
lifting, the alphabets and nets.

And the body—listen—and the
body—who's to say—tossed up

in storm the night before.
Or the gnomon or the hourglass or a comb

drawn slowly through the hair
again and again, the droplets of sweat

intermingling, each one a lens, each a question
visible along the surface of the skin.

But did you ever—do you—did you once—
or then—did you then—nights

(he)—nights
had their sentries and gates,

passages where—decibels—maybe folds where—
and I'm speaking from memory here,

memory could not interfere.
So if the fingers, lunate,

could remember the hand
could account for it

could summon the wrist,
fashion gestures and figures.

And if the hallways and stairs,
the slow flares as they settled

to perplex geometry,
angels invisible at the parapets

and the bent, lettristic acrobats
now deaf, held still and

fearing themselves. And you think
you are making a picture

uttering a sound
saying a thing

and you pretend to wrest the helix from its sleep,
to free its threads

amidst the rubble of the square,
whoever was awake and waiting there.

We pointed toward space
as it is before day.

Disclosures

1

Beneath the writing on the wall
is the writing it was designed

to obscure. The two together
form a third kind

2

There is no writing
on the wall's other side

Perhaps this lack
constitutes a fourth kind

3

Some of the writing on the wall
will be designated as truth

some as art

4

It is said to represent a mirror
of everyday life in its time

5

"Fabius Naso
talks through his asshole

and shits out his mouth"
for example

6

"Foute les Arabes"
for example

7

Certain words and images
or parts of images

have been chipped away
These often turn up for sale

at sidewalk stalls
before the walls

of other cities

8

I too have an image for sale
It's the image of a poem

and is to be found
on the reverse of this sheet

Untitled (Far Away Near)

Still early still late
Have we asked enough questions about space
and what surrounds space
and the hands of a body tumbling through space

Still early still late
as a leaf might curl in a certain way
thinking to turn into carbonized lace
and a body might hurtle through space

Does a color experience pain
while falling through endless space
falling like a blob of sun or a peacock's call
(This June we have no rain at all)

How far away are the voices you hear
and those you can't seem to recall
Does each color recite a name
as if it were its own

yet almost unknowable like a fragrance of plums
(Your house is under repair your house is gone)
Question of the signs the bodies before us form
illegible as dust or eye of noon

Why did the Angel Phosphor arrive
in that city on that (white) night
caduceus held forward in its hand
We had joked that there was no city only winter

no winter only wind
only early and lateness, only streets and blown pages
then the day's final words
traced in silver fluid at the edge of the stage

What then if we spelled "after" with different letters
the letters for "first" or "last," for example
for "forest of burning boats" or "farther"
and it came to mean "the chaos of the waterwheel"

or "the glow of the Thomson lamp"
What if spoken in muteness or danced without memory
What if as elsewhere or blinded, but watching the fire
helix of flames in the center of a square

Have we asked enough questions about changes of light
over time
Use music if you want
Yet let it not reach the ear

                                                    for the dancers

Untitled

O you in that little bark
What is the relation of the painting to its title

The painting bears no relation to its title
The tiny boat bears

nameless people across
water that is infinitely dark

darker even than snow on paving stones
darker than faces in shadow on a boat

The boat is called Blunder, or Nothing, or Parallel Lines
The poem was called I Forget, then Empire, then Game of Cards

a game played yesterday in milky light
light which played across the players' faces

and the arcane faces of the cards
There is no relation between the painting and its title

The painting came first then its title
The players are playing cards in a little boat

They are asleep and it is dark
Their dream is called The Orderly Electrons

One traveler dreams she does not belong
Another dreams with his eyes wide open

like a solemn philosopher
dead from an act of thought

Two more lie with limbs intertwined
The painting has no title

though it has been signed Keeper of the Book
the signature obviously forged

for D.S.

Red Yellow Blue

(Sarah's Eighth)

Now that you know all the words
and I have almost forgotten them

Or now that you have experienced rain
for days on end

and learned to paint with red, yellow and blue
those days which seem to have no end

and I see you often walking alone
down the street or else among friends

mindful of company, equally wondering
wherefrom a world's wrongs stem

And now that you may swim out of sight
if you choose, as choose you must

all along,
a song

Untitled (September '92)

Or maybe this
is the sacred, the vaulted and arched, the
nameless, many-gated
zero where children

where invisible children
where the cries
of invisible children rise
between the Cimetière M

and the Peep Show Sex Paradise
Gate of Sound and Gate of Sand—
Choirs or Mirrors—
Choir like a bundle of tongues

Mirror like a ribbon of tongues
(such that images will remain
once the objects are gone)
Gate of the Body and Gate of the Law

Gate of Public Words, or Passages,
of Suddenness and Cells, Compelling Logic, Gate
of the Hat Filled with Honey
and Coins Bathed in Honey

As the light erases
As heat will etch a d, a design, a
descant of broken lines into glass
Exactly here

between thought and extended arm,
between the gate named for lies
and the double X of the empty sign,
a kind of serous field,

fluid scene or site
peopled with shadows
pissing blood in doorways
yet versed in the mathematics of curves,

theory of colors,
history of time
At Passages we peer out
over a tracery of bridges,

patchwork of sails
At Desire is it possible
we speak without tongues
or see only with tongues

And at Lateness we say
This will be the last
letter you'll receive,
final word you'll hear

from me for now
Is it that a fire
once thought long extinguished
continues to burn

deep within the ground,
a fire finally acknowledged
as impossible to put out,
and that plumes of flame and smoke

will surface at random
enlacing the perfect symmetries
of the Museum of the People
and the Palace of the Book

Or that a Gate of Hours speaks
in a language unfamiliar,
unlike any known,
yet one clear enough

clear as any other
and clear as the liquid
reflection of a gate,
gate whose burnt pages

are blowing through the street
past houses of blue paper
built over fault lines
as if by intent

Untitled (kN)

We made a week of eight days
Each day a new bird spoke

from a bird book, a book of streets and names
codices and vanishings

Each new day we passed the body's name
from hand to hand, eye to ear

according to a script spoken by the ear
on the second day, maybe the third

incomprehensible to us all
in sleep, this promise

or week of promises
and parallel songs

Press your hands everywhere said the songs
to each other back and forth

there's a book infinite as scissors
there's an irreparable book

a fragment like an arm
Let's make a week of eight days

each one the last to itself
each a book uttering a phrase

and each the remnant of one page
from a bird book, a forgotten book

of intervals, a lost book
Run your fingers down the page

Untitled (March '93)

As what's-his-name says in 109, movement three
I went to that favorite magazine store
to find an image
but it was closed

permanently closed it seems
by means of an ancient lock and key,
went to her ear for a word or more
The inclination of her head

beneath the rain instructed me
As David said in a recent letter
the time's about to arrive for someone close
someone I almost know

the false sky has never been this blue
and by blue I mean a specific blue
made of letters I forget—
call it this or that

The train departs during such a period
in such weather: storm from the northwest
lasting as long as a single night
which can't be divided

The two embracing in the courtyard below
must know that even the stars' bond betrays
Still let's happily believe in the figure
for a while. It's enough

Under the Perseids

Even as it passes
we can't make out its name

Yet a river of stone
could have been a river

and the b—the buzz—of blessing
might have been all knowledge

swimming in a blank book
a stone book opened flat

or maybe just a phrase book
where bread translates as bread

felt opposite of itself
and a listing boat—a stone boat—

mistakes its tongue for a sail
An encounter, it says

as if such were as simple
as tossing dust in the air

There is a list, it says, more or less
of what we are, what we own

a window and a door
the steps leading in

These glasses are mine, for example,
this question, the angle of a gaze

the paradise it describes
and the one it denies

A few friends are seated on a verandah
in impossibly heavy air

The music floating up
seems some combination

of theremin and washboard
fiddle and mandolin

We do not believe it
Do we believe instead

in the blue of history,
the flare of a spirit lamp

bridging two bodies,
how the surface of the hand

will imitate a map
Whatever it is

mirror to mirror
that suddenness of crows

tremor as the body opens
always perishing

to Jerry Estrin

Far Away Near

"We link too many things together"
Agnès Rouzier

As it's said in The Fragments
I met the blind typist

inventor of words
The iris of the eye

is an inverted flower
and the essay on snow

offers no beginning
only an aspect of light

beneath a gate
only a photograph of earth

only a fold
a grammar reciting its laws

Just as the clatter
seems distant

and dies without further thought
that moment we ask

Have we reached the center yet, or
Should there be more blue do you think

or just a different shade of blue
all the while tacitly acknowledging

that by blue
she might have meant red

and by red . . .
As it's said

we must train our guns toward the future
where the essay on light will obviate time

and the essay on smoke
will cause the ground to open

One day I completed the final word
of a letter to my father

in what key I forget
After the ink had dried

I noticed the rain lit by a streetlamp
shaped like a conical hat

I noticed the map
of the moon you had left

half in shadow on my desk
In a city near the North Sea

white nights passed as I read
of an aviator downed

in the Barr Adjam
during the war directly after

the war to end all wars
sightless and burned across

three-fourths of his body
Listening in twin silences

his name had disappeared
from his lips

As it's said in The Fragments
There once was a language with two words

and the picture of an apple tree
As it's said

The ravens present a paradox
We learn a new gesture

utter unintelligible sounds
in a cheerful voice perhaps

pointing to the sky
where the rain continues

Autobiography

All clocks are clouds.

Parts are greater than the whole.

A philosopher is starving in a rooming house, while it rains outside.

He regards the self as just another sign.

Winter roses are invisible.

Late ice sometimes sings.

A and *Not-A* are the same.

My dog does not know me.

Violins, like dreams, are suspect.

I come from Kolophon, or perhaps some small island.

The strait has frozen, and people are walking—a few skating—across it.

On the crescent beach, a drowned deer.

A woman with one hand, her thighs around your neck.

The world is all that is displaced.

Apples in a stall at the streetcorner by the Bahnhof, pale yellow to blackish red.

Memory does not speak.

Shortness of breath, accompanied by tinnitus.

The poet's stutter and the philosopher's.

The self is assigned to others.

A room from which, at all times, the moon remains visible.

Leningrad cafe: a man missing the left side of his face.

Disappearance of the sun from the sky above Odessa.

True description of that sun.

A philosopher lies in a doorway, discussing the theory of colors

with himself

the theory of self with himself, the concept of number, eternal return, the sidereal pulse

logic of types, Buridan sentences, the *lekton*.

Why now that smoke off the lake?

Word and thing are the same.

Many times white ravens have I seen.

That all planes are infinite, by extension.

She asks, Is there a map of these gates?

She asks, Is this the one called Passages, or is it that one to the west?

Thus released, the dark angels converse with the angels of light.

They are not angels.

Something else.

for Poul Borum

Autobiography 2 (hellogoodby)

The Book of Company which
I put down and can't pick up

The Trans-Siberian disappearing,
the Blue Train and the Shadow Train

Her body with ridges like my skull
Two children are running through the Lion Cemetery

Five travelers are crossing the Lion Bridge
A philosopher in a doorway insists

that there are no images
He whispers instead: Possible Worlds

The Mind-Body Problem
The Tale of the Color Harpsichord

Skeleton of the World's Oldest Horse
The ring of O dwindles

sizzling round the hole until gone
False spring is laughing at the snow

and just beyond each window
immense pines weighted with snow

A philosopher spread-eagled in the snow
holds out his Third Meditation

like a necrotic star. He whispers:
archery is everywhere in decline,

photography the first perversion of our time
Reach to the milky bottom of this pond

to know the feel of bone,
a knuckle from your grandfather's thumb,

the maternal clavicle, the familiar
arch of a brother's brow

He was your twin, no doubt,
forger of the unicursal maze

My dearest Tania, When I get a good position in the courtyard
I study their faces through the haze

Dear Tania, Don't be annoyed,
please, at these digressions

They are soldering the generals
back onto their pedestals

for A.C.

Index of Titles

Index of First Lines